T0278744

SECRET
NORMANDY

Jean-Christophe Collet and Alain Joubert

IN ASSOCIATION WITH
*Marie Painblanc-Lesobre, Marie-Odile Boitout
and Dominique Krauskopf*

JONGLEZ PUBLISHING

Travel guides

After the success of the French edition, we have taken immense pleasure in updating the *Secret Normandy* guidebook. Through its pages we hope that, like us, you'll continue to discover unusual, secret and lesser-known aspects of the region.

This is a practical guide: all the places mentioned are accessible and clearly marked on the maps that open each chapter. Thematic boxes accompanying certain locations highlight historical points or recount anecdotes that help to reveal all their complexity.

Secret Normandy also showcases numerous details in places that you might pass every day without noticing. These are an invitation to observe the landscape more closely and, in general, offer a way of looking at our locality with the curiosity and attention we often show while travelling ...

We welcome feedback on this guide and its contents, as well as information on places not mentioned here, to enrich future editions.

Feel free to contact us:
email: infos@editionsjonglez.com

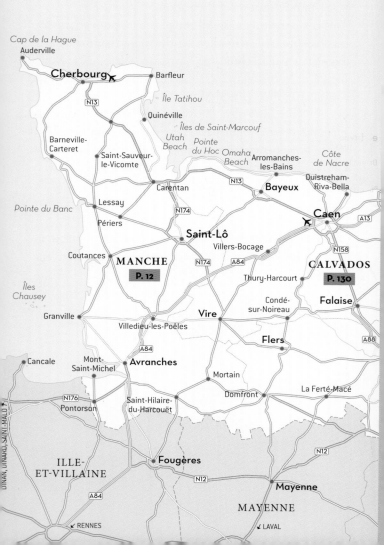

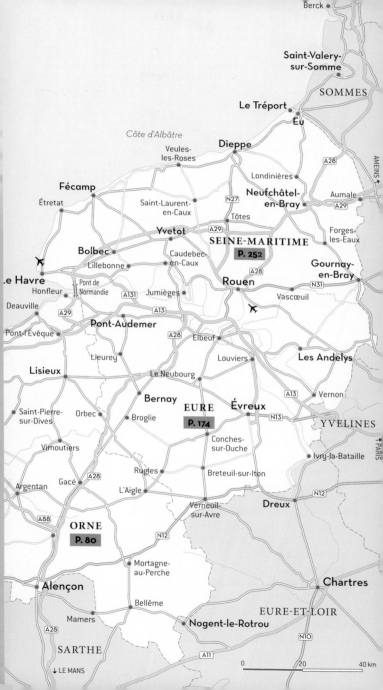

CONTENTS

Manche

Orne

CONTENTS

Calvados

Eure

CONTENTS

Seine-Maritime

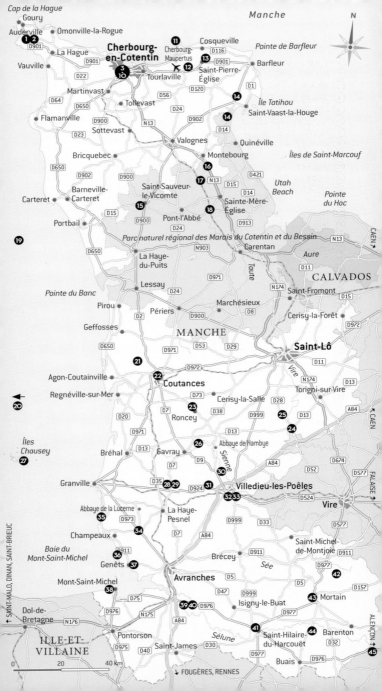

Manche

TOUR OF GROTTES DE JOBOURG

Exploring the depths of the earth

Departure times based on tides
À la Découverte de La Hague association
Excursions mid-July–late Sept
Parking at Nez de Jobourg near La Buvette de la Falaise
50440 Jobourg
02 33 53 86 12 or 06 12 42 86 97
Association Exspen
Mid-July, mid-Feb
Parking at Auberge des Grottes
50440 Jobourg
Cyrille Forafo: 06 31 45 25 80
contact@exspen.com – exspen.com
aladecouvertedelahague@gmail.com – aladecouvertedelahague.fr

The remarkable Jobourg caves, little known to the general public, can be toured with guides from the associations À la Découverte de La Hague and Exspen (Exploration, Sport et Environnement). You descend steep paths along the cliffs, sometimes even roped together, and once your feet touch the shore you still need to crawl on all fours to enter the caverns. It's well worth the effort: the spectacle inside the Grotte du Lion (Lion Cave) and its counterparts is truly magnificent. The walls are covered with lichens that shimmer brightly in the torchlight.

During the walk there's a short detour to the Grotte de l'Église (Church Cave), so named because locals are convinced a passage leads from there to Jobourg church.

NEARBY
On the Smugglers' Trail   ②

'Sur les Traces des Contrebandiers' tour
All year route, 24/7, for at least two people
Bring spare clothes, water, food, non-slip shoes – minimum 5 hours depending on numbers
Parking at Auberge des Grottes
50440 Jobourg
Association Exspen

During the 17th and 18th centuries the Jobourg caves became a hideout for brigands who smuggled their loot back from the nearby Anglo-Norman islands. The caves were largely unaffected by high tides and hard to reach for the customs officers of that time, known as the 'Gabelous'. If you'd like to know more, Cyrille Forafo offers a walk 'On the Smugglers' Trail'. He revives with great aplomb those moments from the 17th to the 19th centuries when The Hague was a major smuggling hotspot. At low tide he'll take you along to explore the iconic routes of these smugglers and tell inside stories of the cliffs, said to be some of the highest in Europe. There's an alternative and more challenging variation of the route called the 'Grand Crapahut', during which you climb and descend for six hours using abseiling techniques. As you near the top of the cliff, towering over 126 metres, take one last look at the bay, the Flamanville headland, and the Anglo-Norman island of Aurigny.

BRÉCOURT ROCKET LAUNCHER

Little-known relics of the Second World War

Brécourt site – Rue Prévert
50120 Cherbourg-en-Cotentin
Open only during Journées de Patrimoine (Heritage Days)

In the 1920s sailors preferred diesel to steam power. Throughout France there was a flurry of activity to find storage facilities. In the Nord-Cotentin region, the French navy set its sights on the Brécourt site in Équeurdreville-Hainneville.

From 1932 to 1938 around 5,000 workers, some of them foreigners, laboured tirelessly to prepare these grounds. Their work was monumental. Beneath the hill they constructed eight concrete tanks with a capacity of 80,000 cubic metres, together with two underground factories.

In 1939 the Second World War broke out and the Germans took over the site to establish a V2 rocket launch site under the direction of Adolf Hitler himself.

At first the Germans planned to install two launching ramps and store 300 missiles (equivalent to around six days of firepower). But the project was ultimately abandoned, as the Third Reich opted for V1 flying bombs. The American army occupied the site on 17 June 1944.

Had the site been operational it would have posed a real threat to Britain, opening up a wide firing angle on the ports and towns between Southampton, Cornwall, Bristol and Cardiff.

You can still see the unfinished launching ramp, lacking its 5-metre-thick roof.

See also the V1 launch site in Seine-Maritime (p. 258).

Apple tree named after Winston Churchill

On the Brécourt site is an apple tree named after Winston Churchill. After the Liberation, Churchill visited Brécourt.
On arriving at the construction site he exclaimed, 'Oh, my God!' Witnesses say he even dropped the apple he was holding. Since that day, according to local legend, the tree has grown under the Normandy sun.

AMERICAN CIVIL WAR GRAVES

Southerners and Northerners buried side by side

Old cemetery – Chemin des Aiguillons
50100 Cherbourg-en-Cotentin
Open daily 9am–6pm

The old cemetery of La Duché, built in 1825 and expanded in 1926, holds around 13,000 graves spread over an area of nearly 10 hectares. The oldest lie between Boulevard Guillaume le Conquérant and Chemin des Aiguillons. The cemetery with its white concrete headstones is the last resting place of 86 British airmen from the First World War. This is also one of the few places in the world where opponents in a civil war lie side by side – specifically American sailors from USS *Kearsarge* and CSS *Alabama*.

In June 1864 the two warships from the Southern (Confederate) and Northern (Federal) navies played their last role in the American Civil War off the coast of Cherbourg. On 11 June CSS *Alabama*, a Confederate ship, entered the port of Nord-Cotentin for a repairs

stopover. Under the eyes of the people of Cherbourg, the 22-month voyage of the 66-metre three-masted ship came to an end.

CSS *Alabama* was considered the most efficient warship of the Confederate navy. Under the command of Admiral Raphael Semmes, 65 Union vessels were captured in the Azores, the Gulf of Mexico, off the coast of Brazil, and even in Singapore. The warship, docked in Cherbourg, awaited authorisation from Emperor Napoleon III to make repairs as quickly as possible. But the order never came. On 14 June a Union cruiser, USS Kearsarge commanded by Captain John Winslow, finally appeared a short distance from the Cherbourg coastline.

On the morning of Sunday 19 June CSS *Alabama* left port, escorted by armoured frigate La Couronne, to meet its adversary. Outside French territorial waters they weren't alone, as onlookers and journalists had hired small boats to witness the anticipated naval battle.

The sailors of both ships fought mercilessly, exchanging cannon fire for 90 minutes. Far from their homelands, 26 of them lost their lives in this fierce confrontation, after which CSS *Alabama* surrendered and sank with all hands. The wreck was discovered by the minehunter *Circé* a century later, in 1984, lying at a depth of 60 metres off the coast of Querqueville.

Since 1988, annual excavations have been carried out at the site under the leadership of a navy captain.

FONTAINE DES CAVALIERS

A fountain that was once a washbasin

Rue Emmanuel Liais, 50100 Cherbourg-en-Cotentin

In the 18th century a fountain fed by the Polle stream was built on Rue Christine. But in August 1788, due to traffic congestion at the intersection with Rue de l'Abbaye, local officials decided to relocate and rebuild it on Rue Emmanuel Liais. The Knights' Fountain is a granite basin featuring a stele of limestone from the Yvetot region of Seine-Maritime. The pediment, depicting the town coat of arms within a crowned shield surrounded by two palm fronds and cornucopias, was carved by Cherbourg artist François-Armand Fréret. The basin was used for washing until the 1950s.

NEARBY

Courvoisier ad for 'The brandy of Napoleon' ⑥

56, quai de Caligny
50100 Cherbourg-en-Cotentin

Napoleon, on his way into exile on the island of Saint Helena, is said to have taken bottles of the famous Courvoisier cognac with him. The manufacturer has since used this notoriety in its advertising.

One of these ads can still be seen at No. 56 Quai de Caligny. Painted on the gable of a building, it carries the slogan 'The brandy of Napoleon'.

LES GALERIES 117

Unique underground tunnels

Association Exspen
1 Rue Fernand Thomine
50100 Cherbourg-en-Cotentin
Tours in groups of 18
Cyrille Forafo: 06 31 45 25 80 – contact@exspen.com

Fort du Roule was constructed under Louis XVI and Napoleon as part of the military port of Cherbourg. In the late 1920s the French built galleries at its base to store ammunition and torpedoes.

In 1940 the Germans took over the site to make it an essential part of the Atlantic Wall. They dug an additional tunnel and installed batteries on the northern flank of the mountain.

From 1940 to 1944 over a hundred soldiers lived in the fort to monitor the harbour and operate the four powerful batteries. On 22 June 1944 the Americans decided to bombard Le Roule site through concentrated air and ground attacks.

The abandoned galleries were sealed off by the navy. They can now be seen, guided by Cyrille Forafo, on an underground walking tour with commentary. Visitors will be accompanied and supplied with caving helmet and headlamp to explore over 700 metres of tunnels, four batteries armed with 105 mm cannons, and a command post.

The site, classified as a Historic Monument, is highlighted by quality scenography. It contributes to commemorating a region marked by the Second World War as well as offering breathtaking views of the harbour and Vauban's 17th-century military fortifications. A revealing insight into Cherbourg history.

German forces surrendering to American troops in front of the entrance to Fort du Roule galleries.

OMNIA CINEMA MURALS

20th-century heritage murals

Cinéma Omnia
12 Rue de la Paix – 50100 Cherbourg-en-Cotentin
Visits: call Mairie de Cherbourg during office hours: 02 33 87 88 62, ask for
Monsieur Barbarin

The *Omnia* cinema, operated from the outset by the renowned Pathé company, opened on 28 September 1911 featuring the film *La Révolte de Redwood* (Redwood revolt) as part of its programme. It screened many feature films, including one made in 1946 at The Hague by Henri Calef and known as *La Maison sous la mer* (The house under the sea).

In 1952, the building was entirely renovated by the intervention of Cherbourg resident Jean Métivier. At the opening of the new layout, the cinema screened *Un Grand patron* (*Perfectionist*) on 21 March 1952, directed by Yves Ciampi and starring Pierre Fresnay. Following the customs of that time, the feature film was preceded by two documentaries, one about the Amazon and the other about the navy in Indochina.

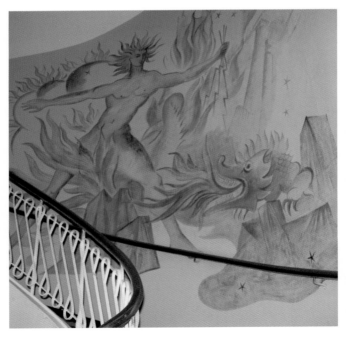

For many years the *Omnia* was Cherbourg's leading cinema, attracting over 117,000 admissions in its heyday (and 80,000 in the 1980s). It was taken over by the town in 1986 and converted into a public venue.

The interior murals by R. Lecoq were honoured in 2006 with the Patrimoine XXᵉ Siècle (20th-Century Heritage) label from the Ministry of Culture. The murals are inspired by mythology. The one at the entrance depicts Aeolus and Vulcan, and on the walls surrounding the screen are Neptune and Amphitrite.

The art deco style of the fully glazed facade with its blue borders stands out from the other buildings on the street. A wooden ticket booth is tucked in between two spiral staircases, as well as two sets of stone steps leading to the mezzanine balcony.

EXCERPT FROM *MÉMORIAL DE SAINTE-HÉLÈNE*

'I had resolved to recreate the wonders of Egypt in Cherbourg'

Place Napoléon
50100 Cherbourg-en-Cotentin

The equestrian statue of Napoleon I, erected in the square named after him, is the work of Armand Le Véel (born in Bricquebec in 1821, died in 1905), a pupil of patriotic sculptor François Rude. Napoleon's illustrious figure is depicted contemplating the harbour and military port.

A close look reveals an excerpt from his *Memorial of Saint Helena* on the statue's pedestal: *J'avais résolu de renouveler à Cherbourg les merveilles de l'Egypte* (I had resolved to recreate the wonders of Egypt in Cherbourg).

The French emperor wanted to build a pyramid, the Napoleon battery, in the centre of the main dike, and an artificial lake for the harbour in memory of the legendary Lake Moeris excavated by Herodotus in Egypt. The statue was unveiled on 4 August 1858 by Napoleon III in the presence of Queen Victoria and Prince Albert. Several other events took place: opening of the Paris-Cherbourg train line by Napoleon III himself, commissioning a new basin, and strengthening the entente cordiale with the United Kingdom. This Cherbourg icon, classified as a Historic Monument since 31 January 2008, demonstrates Napoleon's interest in the town's expansion.

Contrary to what is often believed, Napoleon is pointing with his right arm towards the military port, not towards England: *The hand that builds and not the one that threatens*, as stated by Léon Favier in *Mémoires de la Société nationale académique de Cherbourg*.

NEARBY

Bust of the most Napoleonic Cherbourgeois ⑩

A bust was erected on 12 May 1850 on Quai de Caligny in honour of Colonel de Bricqueville, a prominent Cherbourg military figure who had strong ties with Napoleon. He was a colonel of the Imperial Dragoons and a Bonapartist deputy of Cherbourg. The bronze sculpture, 1.45 metres high, was created by renowned artist David d'Angers. It stands on a 4-metre granite column designed by architect Lemelle and bears the names of the Napoleonic battles where Colonel de Bricqueville showed courage: Wagram, Krasnoe, Anvers, Versailles. The bust is listed as a Historic Monument.

PORT PIGNOT

One of the smallest ports in France

Fermanville tourist office
20 La Vallée des Moulins
50640 Fermanville – on D116
02 33 23 12 13

Port Pignot at Fermanville, a charming village with several windmills, has to be one of the smallest ports in France. But unlike Port Racine, which is known to tourists in the nearby La Hague region, it's very quiet and less frequented. The 19 pleasure boats moored here, near Cap Lévi, are crammed into a space of 30 by 30 metres. Protected from the swells by rocky embankments, the port was devised in 1889 by Charles Pignot, who operated a nearby quarry. Barges loaded with the renowned Fermanville pink granite would embark from here.

On leaving Pignot you can discover the six other ports of Val de Saire: Le Becquet (95 berths), Port Lévi (80 berths), Roubari (31 berths), Barfleur (140 moorings), and Saint-Vaast-la-Hougue (700 berths).

While all of these now accommodate pleasure boats, only Barfleur is still an active fishing port.

Pink granite of Fermanville

Fermanville's pink granite, in use since the 15th century, was renowned for its high quality and large feldspar crystals. It was used to build the adjoining viaduct. This stone also forms part of the slipway for the Compagnie Générale Transatlantique in Le Havre dating from 1914, the facade of Printemps department store in Paris, the commemorative obelisk at Utah Beach, and numerous war memorials. The quarry is no longer in operation.

Drink elderflower!

Elderberry is a remarkable tree with multiple uses. Its flowers produce a delicious sparkling beverage that can be found in summer at Fermanville market. The fruit is also worth discovering as jam or jelly. Local children, crafting whistles from elderberry wood, have clearly fallen for these delicious products.

© Martin Leveneur

TOMB OF GENEVIÈVE LAMACHE

The grave of an adopted daughter of Napoleon

Carneville cemetery
50330 Carneville

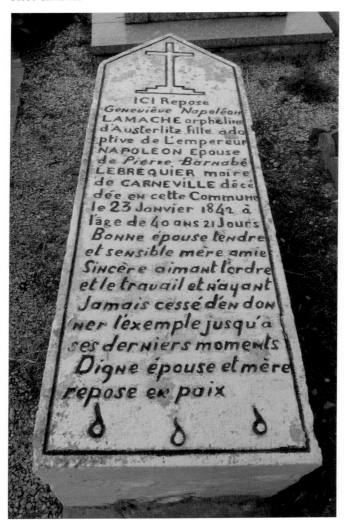

This remarkable tombstone epitaph In Carneville cemetery translates as: 'Here lies Geneviève Napoléon Lamache, orphan of Austerlitz, adopted daughter of the Emperor Napoleon.' By decree, Napoleon had indeed adopted all the children of the generals, officers and soldiers lost at Austerlitz. Geneviève Napoléon Lamache, who died at the age of 40 in 1842, was one of the countless children who were 'adopted' by the emperor. Her father, Martin Lamache, was a corporal in the Napoleonic *Grande Armée*. Born in 1780 at Clitourps, he followed the 'great army' from the camp of Boulogne-sur-Mer to Austria, covering 30–40 km per day. He was seriously injured during the battle and died at the hospital in Brünn (Brno) in December 1805. There is another Napoleonic relic at Théville in Val de Saire – a war memorial in memory of Bonaparte's soldiers.

NEARBY
Saint-Pierre-Église's 13 lavoirs ⑬
50530 Saint-Pierre-Église

For centuries, *lavoirs* (washhouses or laundries) were the meeting places for gossip and social interaction. The best-known washerwoman in Manche was Mère Denis, who gained fame through the advertising campaign for the *Vedette* brand in the 1970s (see p. 159). In the past, there were three stages to clean laundry: hell (passing through the trough), purgatory (beating the laundry) and paradise (rinsing, wringing, drying). In Saint-Pierre-Église, 13 washhouses have been identified by historians, including the one in Raffoville. But similar ones can be found in all Val de Saire villages.

GRAFFITI IN MORSALINES AND QUETTEHOU CHURCHES

Tags of erstwhile sailors

50630 Quettehou

Graffiti art was a popular form of expression when people were less literate, as a pastime or to share maritime feelings. In Normandy, they were typically made at a reachable height on relatively soft stones. They often chronicled the lives of fishermen and labourers who were sometimes forcibly recruited onto royal ships.

Within places of worship these 'tags' from the past were considered as ex-votos, seeking God's protection against the dangers of the sea. Today they provide an interesting iconography of Norman ships before the 18th century.

These graffiti, by sailors rather than artists, weren't meant for aesthetic effect. They represent the essential characteristics of various types of vessel such as warships, frigates, brigs and schooners, as well as fishing and merchant ships with round sterns, including galiots, flutes, flibots, doggers, sloops and cutters.

Graffiti of this kind are uncommon on buildings or churches in Lower Normandy. They can be found along the banks of the Seine, Eure, Orne, Touques and Dives rivers.

In Val de Saire, Quettehou and Tatihou churches have a few of these graffiti. In Morsalines there are engravings of ship drawings on the outside walls of the church. The most interesting is on a pillar at the entrance to the cemetery, along Avenue de la Peinterie

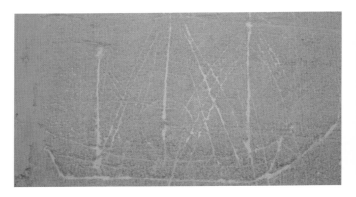

MAIRIE DE REIGNEVILLE

A town hall in a sacristy

50390 Reigneville-Bocage

Reigneville is as picturesque and tranquil a village as you could wish for. Some distance from Cherbourg, it lacks basic amenities such as a school, cemetery, bar, bakery or butcher's shop. You won't even find a village square here.

In Reigneville the residents lead a peaceful life in old stone houses scattered throughout the *bocage* (mixed woodland and meadows) and hidden behind leafy embankments. It's a place of utmost tranquillity. The only monthly event that brings the villagers together is their local council meeting, held in a former sacristy now used as the town hall.

To find the hall, follow the directions on a small wooden sign, take a dirt path until you reach a farmyard. The building, standing amidst meadows with its white door, beautiful wayside cross, and a sign reading '*mairie*', isn't very big. You might find it hard to imagine that this was once a church where worshippers gathered. Voices are no longer hushed when it comes to today's decisions on roadworks or votes on the budget!

Before leaving the village, it's worth taking a short detour via the 16th-century manor with brick turret, just behind the farmhouse. A fine testament to the Renaissance.

AIRSHIP HANGAR

Unique in France

50310 Écausseville
Exit route national at Écausseville and follow signs
For opening hours contact 02 33 08 56 02,
Montebourg tourist office: 02 33 41 15 73
or Jacques Hochet: 02 33 41 15 73

Although the airship hangar dominates the view near the small village of Écausseville, when first seen from a car you have the curious impression of moving away from it ...

But after a few determined minutes on winding country roads you'll arrive in front of the imposing iron and concrete cathedral-like structure. Measuring 150 metres in length, 40 metres in width and 30 metres in height, it was completed in 1919, well after the Armistice.

The hangar was designed by Swiss civil engineer Henri Lossier and built by Fourré et Rhodes enterprises. The original purpose was to house airships used to detect German submarine attacks on Allied commercial traffic. In 1936 the French navy, owner of the site, definitively abandoned the use of these airships.

The hangar, occupied for four years by the mobile coastal artillery and anti-aircraft group, was requisitioned from 1940 to 1944 by the German army. Some graffiti signed by Wehrmacht soldiers can still be found here and there.

After the Liberation, the Americans found this imposing structure to their liking and converted it to a warehouse for storing equipment. The French navy subsequently used it to park vehicles until the late 1990s.

The hangar, covered with 3,500 tiles, is now classified as a Historic Monument and is one of the last survivors of the 12 airship centres built during the First World War (there's another in Meudon, near Paris – see *Grand Paris insolite et secret*, also published by Jonglez).

The Association des Amis du Hangar à Dirigeables d'Écausseville, which manages the site, now aims to preserve it from the ravages of time. They also intend to set up a centre for airship activities, accommodating tourism, transport and ULM (ultra-light motorised) events.

According to the association's president, Philipe Belin, around 4 million euros still need to be raised to restore the military behemoth. But there's no longer any question of the monument becoming a museum of American aviation.

MUSÉE DE L'HORLOGERIE

Space-time in a museum

Chateau de Potteries – 50310 Fresville
06 30 26 21 32
Daily 2pm–6pm

In March 2002, in Fresville, a group of enthusiasts founded the Association of Antique Watch Collectors. Time went by ... and in May 2008, their president opened a small clockmaking museum in Potteries castle. The collection is remarkable. In addition to watches, a section is dedicated to Comtoise weight-driven clocks with intricate structural movements.

The forgotten heritage of horology is highly appreciated by foreigners, who seek out Norman lantern clocks dating from the 17th to the 19th centuries in particular. While exploring the museum, take a moment to admire a small Swiss clock from 1606 and a complicated movement indicating the days, date, months and lunar phases. Round off your visit with the fully reconstructed 20th-century clockmaker's workshop.

La Hague, a film set

Brochure available at La Hague tourist office
Several hiking trails are on offer to explore the film sets
La Hague tourist office: 45 Rue Jallot, 50440 La Hague
02 33 52 74 34

The Hague has inspired several filmmakers. Roman Polanski chose the Manoir du Tourp Manor to film *Tess*, and Jean-Claude Brialy shot *Un bon petit diable* (A good little devil) in Flamanville in 1983. In the same village, Florence Moncorgé-Gabin filmed *Le Passager de l'été* (The summer traveller) in 2005, starring Catherine Frot, François Berléand, Mathilde Seigner and Laura Smet.

In 1947, Henri Calef wielded his camera in Flamanville and Diélette for his feature film *La Maison sous la mer*, inspired by Paul Vialar's novel, with Anouk Aimée playing her first major role on the big screen.

Two years later, in 1949, Yves Allégret directed Gérard Philippe and Madeleine Robinson in *Une si jolie petite plage* (Such a pretty little beach).

In 1950, in *La Marie au port* (Mary at the port), it was Marcel Carné's turn to film Jean Gabin at Saint-Vaast-La-Hougue and Cherbourg.

And last but not least, don't forget the most famous film, *The Longest Day* (1962). Directed by Ken Annakin, Bernhard Wicki and Andrew Marton, it was set in Sainte-Mère-Église and featured John Wayne, Paul Anka, Sean Connery and Henry Fonda.

The list wouldn't be complete without mentioning *Les Parapluies de Cherbourg* (The Umbrellas of Cherbourg), award-winner at Cannes. Jacques Demy had brought Catherine Deneuve to Cherbourg.

RED-PAINTED CASTLE AT CHEF-DU-PONT

The most expensive artwork in the world?

50480 Sainte-Mère-Église

Near Sainte-Mère-Église, the facade of Château du Val, dating back to the 18th century, no longer attracts much attention. Its red door is the only surviving witness of an eccentricity that once made it famous.

According to the owners it had vied for the title of 'the most expensive artwork in the world' after being completely repainted in vibrant red one fine morning in October 2009.

In charge of the operation was none other than Banksy, commissioned by Mark, Phil and Guy Berridge, the owners of the building, to turn it into a unique production, as suggested by the barcode that looks like prison bars that he'd applied to the wall.

The objective of this stunt? To auction off the dilapidated castle, restore it, and convert it into an ideas laboratory. The alternative collective Common Sense Manifesto, run by Mark Berridge, supported

the operation through a website where anyone could become a buyer. Despite being listed for sale at 1 billion euros, the castle struggled to find a taker ...

While the artist, who expressed a desire to 'awaken people from their stupor by capturing their attention', undoubtedly succeeded in his endeavour, the same can't be said for the owners, who have since been ordered by the local authorities to restore the castle to its original colours.

Indeed, without a building permit not even the most famous graffiti artist had citizens' rights. The following year the stones of the building were sandblasted while the cement was covered with stone-coloured paint.

ÉCRÉHOU ISLANDS

A little paradise on the sea

Anglo-Norman archipelago, off the Channel coast
Shuttles between Barneville and Jersey by Manche Îles Express company
Shuttles from Jersey to Écréhou by Jersey Walk Adventures company
For further information: +44 (0)77 9785 3033
info@jerseywalkadventures.co.uk

Not many have had the chance to set foot on Écréhou, this Anglo-Norman strip of land In the English Channel, 11 km north-east of Jersey and a little less than 15 km off the French coast of Cotentin, near Portbail.

While fishermen from Barneville or Portbail can theoretically take you there, the best way to reach the islands is a shuttle to Jersey and then a small, fast boat to your destination. On arrival you'll no doubt be surprised by the houses clinging to the rocks, sometimes in tatters from the pounding storms.

The houses, owned by the Lord of Rozel and 20 other Jersey islanders and always authentically rebuilt, lend a certain charm to this archipelago to be appreciated slowly. Visitors landing at Marmotière island's small jetty will discover a seaside hamlet, intersected by Rue des Notaires and Place Royal, where the tax offices and the ports ministry are located.

Facing the vastness of the sea, take time out to sit on the only bench on Marmotière island, below the Union Jack. The flag was donated to the residents by islander Herbert William Noel in 1976.

Then continue towards Grande Brecque and its solitary house, and towards Bianque Isle. To reach them, a passage opens at low tide through a bank of pebbles bordered by turquoise sea and brown algae-covered rocks.

Priory on the island

In the 14th and 15th centuries monks from Abbaye de Val Richer, near Lisieux, lived in a priory on the main island of Écréhou archipelago. Some remains still stand today. Making your way through brambles, cormorant nests and tall grass, you can reach the site and appreciate the hardships of their existence.

Écréhou flag

In the early morning it's customary for the first person awake to hoist the flag at the top of the only mast on Marmotière island. 'The flag is never the same,' jokes a Norman historian. It all depends on the mood of whoever is entrusted with the delicate mission. Some days, the Union Jack (the British flag) flies in the wind, but on other days, the Jersey colours flutter at the sky, and sometimes it's the tricolour. This was the case when the flag was raised by a group of French fishermen who, a few years ago, demanded the right to fish Écréhou waters.

Stories set in stone

The Écréhou islands, along with all the Channel Islands and the Cotentin region, were annexed to the Duchy of Normandy in 933. After William the Conqueror and the conquest of England in 1066, the islands became part of Anglo-Norman territory and weren't claimed by French king Philip Augustus during his annexation of the duchy in 1204.

In the 19th century the Écréhous (like Minquiers island – see following double-page spread), became landmarks for smugglers who hid goods such as textiles, wool, lead, tin, tobacco and alcohol, which they sought to clandestinely introduce into France or Jersey. France first claimed sovereignty over these rocks in 1886. In 1950, the matter was brought before the International Court of Justice at The Hague, which confirmed on 17 November 1953 that the Écréhou and Minquiers islands were indeed dependencies of Jersey and the British Crown.

Frenchmen have twice sought the title of Lord of Écréhou. The first was Philippe Pinel, who lived on Blanche Île from 1848 to 1898, and the second was Alphonse Le Gastelois, who took refuge on Marmotière and lived there for 14 years in the 1960s and 1970s (see opposite page).

In 1993 and again in 1994, the French from Normandy took possession of the islands, raised the Norman flag and held a Mass, symbolically protesting against the new fishing zone regulations in the Channel.

Alphonse Le Gastelois: the hermit who didn't wash for 14 years

Born in Jersey on 9 October 1914, Alphonse Le Gastelois couldn't bear the false rumours accusing him of child sexual assault. He left his native Jersey for the Écréhou islands, where he lived from 1961 to April 1975. Despite the eventual arrest of the actual perpetrator, the man who'd been nicknamed 'The Beast of Jersey' said 20 years later: 'Jersey crucified me.'

'He was an original, solitary and peculiar man,' insists a historian who happened on him during his nautical wanderings. 'He spoke French, English and Jèrriais (Jersey dialect) equally well. But when he wasn't in the mood for conversation, you had to leave him alone.'

Far from the mainland, Alphonse lived in the 'huts' of Marmotière, lent to him by the locals. He survived mainly on supplies brought by the French and Jersey people, as well as his fishing. Always wearing his legendary woollen cap and smoking a pipe, the man with dubious cleanliness (he didn't wash for 14 years) officially claimed the title Lord of Écréhou from Queen Elizabeth II, evoking old Norman rights.

Once again wrongly accused, this time for a house fire, he left the archipelago definitively and lived at the expense of the Jersey government. Alphonse Le Gastelois passed away in June 2012.

MINQUIERS

'Do not scorn your dream, for it contains the purpose of your soul'

Anglo-Norman archipelago
45 km off the coast of Barneville
To hire a boat, contact the following:
In Granville: Le Lys Noir old rig – 06 37 33 32 65, contact@lysnoir.fr
In Barneville-Carteret: Cap Nautic – 02 33 01 20 01 (motorboat hire on a daily basis)

There's no public transport to the stunning Minquiers island, a remote Anglo-Norman territory in the Channel. Sailboats will take approximately 4 hours to reach the island from Granville, but it's about 2 hours less from Barneville-Carteret (and a little over an hour by motorboat from Barneville). Anchoring a short distance from the island, where the emerald water hints at pristine depths, visitors can reach the main island by dinghy.

The welcome is 'so British' on arrival at the slipway. A British resident jokingly asks for passports, although the handshake that goes with the words speaks volumes about the joy of receiving visitors.

The 'explorers' are greeted by a rather reserved atmosphere as they reach the top of the slipway. Ten small houses with British residents seemingly pretend not to notice the visitors. Skirting around their stone dwellings, a narrow alley leads to the southernmost toilets in the British Isles, as indicated on the door. Not far away, a rocky promontory overlooks the archipelago, stretching as far as the eye can see at low tide.

Unlike neighbouring Chausey island, Minquiers can be taken in with a single glance. But what a sight! At your feet, sandy expanses and rocky islets emerge from the depths, shaping a landscape unlike any other.

This is neither Chausey, Jersey nor Guernsey. You're simply far from the world, in the realm of shore fishermen and bass fishing. As you leave the archipelago there may be a slight pang of nostalgia, quickly soothed by the spectacle of the ocean with dolphins playing and the luminous reflection of the setting sun on the waves.

Suddenly, you may feel like following the inscription boldly written on a Minquiers rock: 'Do not scorn your dream, for it contains the purpose of your soul.'

Southernmost toilets in the British Isles

The little bunker that often intrigues walkers arriving on Minquiers is a public toilet. The door bears the message: 'This toilet has the distinction of being the most southern building in the British Isles. Please use with care! As the nearest alternative is Jersey 11 miles Chausey 10 miles,' emphasising the importance of preserving these facilities, given their status.

Minquiers, Northern Patagonia

On 31 May 1984 French explorer and travel writer Jean Raspail landed on Minquiers island to hoist the flag of the Kingdom of Patagonia in honour of its deposed (self-proclaimed) king, Antoine de Tounens, a French lawyer and adventurer. On that day Minquiers was baptised 'Northern Patagonia' and the main island was named Port de Tounens.

The exercise, carried out with a commando unit of 13 men, was non-military in nature but still received significant attention from the English press. Raspail did it again in 1998, and the flag of Patagonia was once again raised in place of the Union Jack.

Later on, the flag was handed over to the British Embassy in Paris by Raspail acting as Consul General of the Kingdom of Araucanía and Patagonia in France. Since these two expeditions, the Jersey government has erected beacons in the archipelago and set up a plaque in memory of Monsieur Le Masurier (see below), great saviour of Minquiers and of British sovereignty!

Expeditionary force led by an artist

On 10 June 1939 a group of 36 fishermen led by Marin-Marie, official French navy artist, shipowner Lucien Ernouf from Granville, and Captain Charles Plessis, landed on Minquiers to assert French sovereignty over the archipelago. Their goal was simple: they wanted to build a cabin for Granville fishermen and force the Jersey residents to yield.

The Frenchmen erected a small cabin on the main island in three days. Everything seemed to be going smoothly until an unwelcome visitor, Monsieur Le Masurier, alerted the French authorities to their presence.

There was a flurry of activity on the mainland. The maritime prefect of Cherbourg sent a seaplane over the island to drop a message to Marin-Marie: 'Please stop immediately the work being carried out on the island. The French government alone has the authority to decide on the appropriateness of these activities.'

Following this diplomatic incident, which stemmed from ongoing conflicts between fishermen from Chausey and Jersey, in 1950 France and the United Kingdom brought their sovereignty dispute before the International Court of Justice at The Hague. But it wasn't not until three years later, in 1953, that the Court unanimously ruled against France.

ERMITAGE DE SAINT-GERBOLD

To alleviate digestive disorders ...

Ermitage de Saint-Gerbold
50219 Gratot
Just before Gratot, coming from Coutances, follow signs
Guided tours available during Heritage Days

Just a stone's throw from Château de Gratot, the site of the hermitage of Saint-Gerbold is accessible throughout the year, although the interior is only open to visitors during Heritage Days.

Access is by a small, shaded path. The building, now a Historic Monument, was erected by the local lords and dedicated to the Bishop of Bayeux, St Gerbold. This 7th-century cleric, born in Calvados, worked as a steward for a wealthy English lord. Wrongly accused of seducing the lord's mistress, he was tied to a millstone and thrown into the water. But instead of sinking, the stone saved him and cast him onto the shores of Saint-Ver-sur-Mer.

After becoming Bishop of Bayeux he was expelled from town.

Out of spite, he threw his episcopal ring into a stream, threatening the entire country with dysentery. A fisherman found the object in the belly of a fish, the religious man became a bishop again, and stomach ailments magically disappeared. From then on the holy man was petitioned for all digestive troubles.

The hermitage, built between 1403 and 1418 by Philippe d'Argouges, was initially a chapel where Mass was celebrated by the Gratot priest. Hermits were only taken in from the 17th century. Eight of them succeeded each other until 1830. The best known was Brother Gilles de Saint-Joseph, who wrote a compendium for Lord Louis d'Argouges.

SAINT-PIERRE CEMETERY

A cemetery open once a year

Rue de Geoffroy de Montbray
50200 Coutances
Open only on All Saints' Day

The small Saint-Pierre cemetery at Coutances, rightly considered the burial ground of notables, is home to memorials to some famous residents. In an attempt to prevent vandalism, the site has been open only once a year since 1980. It's a romantic place where visitors will be charmed by the dense vegetation and ivy covering the tombstones embedded in the ground. Closely surrounded by houses, the cemetery saw its last burial in 1995, and has since remained as it has been for centuries. On All Saints' Day you can pay your respects to the distinguished members of the Jean-Jacques Quesnel–Morinière family, laid to rest in a tomb built by the townsfolk in 1853 (see below). A little further and you can bow before the martyrs of the Revolution, including Father Pierre-André Toulorge, guillotined at Coutances in 1793 and beatified in April 2012 in Coutances cathedral.

The Frémin family from Mesnil, long buried there, can also be found. One of them, Gabriel François, served as mayor from 1811 to 1816. His vault is just a stone's throw from the Quesnel-Canveaux family. One of them set up the local charitable office, and another sold his mansion to open place de Parvis in Coutances.

Jean-Jacques Quesnel de la Morinière, Coutances benefactor

Descended from a family of magistrates, Jean-Jacques Quesnel de la Morinière (1765–1852) was a benefactor of the town of Coutances. In 1823 he bought Gabriel d'Ouessey's property and gardens, where he lived happily. In January 1852 he donated this site on the condition that the gardens become a communal park with medicinal plants. As a token of appreciation, mayor Monsieur Brohier-Littinière erected an obelisk in his honour at the centre of the park.

LETENNEUR MAUSOLEUM

An extravagant mausoleum in a peaceful Norman village

50210 Roncey
02 33 46 93 35
mairieroncey@wanadoo.fr
Roncey is about 10 km south-east of Coutances
Follow D7 towards Gavray, then take D76 towards Roncey
Access to mausoleum signposted in village
Open access

The modest village of La Rousserie, about 10 km from Coutances, is home to an extraordinary burial site, completely incongruous in the verdant countryside. Auguste Letenneur lies in this immense structure, standing about 30 metres tall, halfway between a fortress and an ancient temple. It may not be the most discreet final resting place, but the man was eccentric and then some ...

He was born in 1832 in this remote countryside into a humble working family and did various odd jobs on nearby farms before finding his calling: selling canvas and cloth as a travelling merchant. At that time the market was prosperous, and young Auguste quickly abandoned door-to-door sales to buy a store, first in Saint-Lô, then in other major towns throughout the western region. This marked the beginning of an irresistible rise, both commercially and socially. As the dawn of the 20th-century industrial revolution approached, the Letenneur family, and especially its patriarch, became a success symbol.

Self-taught, with literary and poetic inclinations, Letenneur amassed a rich library in his La Rousserie estate and had undertaken to write his life story. However, he only produced a brief and naive poem in praise of his native land.

In 1900 he vowed to be buried on his own ground, and the construction of the family vault began. For the locals who view it with a mixture of amusement and respect, Auguste's project is absolutely grandiose. The crypt, complete with fortified tower, holds his tomb as well as those of his wife and children. A dining room is dedicated to the heirs' meals during family celebrations. A room of contemplation is used for prayers and services. Finally, another tower with a terrace offers a breathtaking view of the surrounding countryside. Auguste Letenneur passed away in 1916, the victim of a farming accident.

La Rousserie mausoleum, abandoned and on the verge of ruin, was bequeathed to the commune by heirs who didn't know what to do with such a burden. Since then volunteers have taken on the task of restoring and rehabilitating the crypt. So rather like Le Palais Idéal built by French postman Ferdinand (Facteur) Cheval over 33 years, the extravagant burial site of wealthy merchant Auguste Letenneur brings a touch of madness to the tranquillity of an ordinary Norman village.

BEE WALL
AT TESSY-BOCAGE

The largest known bee wall in France

Place known as La Poëmellière
50420 Tessy-Bocage
From Tessy-Bocage head towards Chevry and after 2 km turn right into hamlet
For further information contact Gendrin family: 02 33 56 23 70

At the place known as La Poëmellière, the Gendrin family owns the largest known bee wall in France. This beekeeping structure, built by one of their ancestors in the 19th century, is exceptionally large and contains 34 compartments.

Signs along the road point the way to Chevry. Once there, open the gate to a flower-filled garden and behold the wall, which was originally thatched. However, due to the nearby cows eating a substantial portion of the thatch, it has now been replaced with a tin roof.

In Normandy, constructions of this kind were common and made of local stone (schist or limestone). They housed multiple beehives. Less affluent farmers would construct straw beehives without a top, allowing them to smoke out the bees safely.

NEARBY
Grotte au diable

50420 Fervaches

Amédée Duval-Dupeyron, a magistrate in Tessy during the 19th century, was by no means a hermit but enjoyed solitude and reading. To isolate himself from the world, he converted the 'devil's cave' into a reading room. The cave in the woods wasn't chosen at random by the magistrate. It overlooks the Vire river winding its way below. Access to the cave is via the GR221 hiking trail and the towpath, following a small path secured with safety rails.

WHALEBONE ENIGMA

An odd name

Église de La Baleine
50028 La Baleine
Access via D13: head towards La Baleine from Saint-Denis-le-Gast
Church open daily, late in the morning; if you arrive early key to building can
be obtained from Auberge du Krill

La Baleine, a charming and picturesque village in the Normandy countryside, nestled in a green valley, doesn't quite live up to its name. After all, this hamlet is far from the Atlantic Ocean and huge cetaceans. Norman specialists have a string of hypotheses to explain this. Albert Dauzat, along with Auguste Longnon and Auguste Vincent, believe that the village's name is a deformation of the legacy of Gallic goddess Belisma. But this version is now generally disputed. Another scholar, François de Beaurepaire, offers a much simpler explanation. The name is said to derive from a lost anecdote. The most plausible and interesting explanation, as favoured by Ernest Nègre, sees it as the feminine adjectival form of the Old French word *balain*, which meant 'land of broom'. The locals have their own opinions. Some suggest that the name comes from *ballaine*, meaning 'valley', while others claim that Granville sailors built a chapel there to thank God for rescuing them from a shipwreck.

The village's relatively recent church is dedicated to St Peter. It was built between the 12th and 19th centuries, and the square tower with four gables lends plenty of character. For centuries the votive offering of a whale rib has been displayed inside the chapel without anyone knowing where it came from.

According to mayor Bernard Lejeune, the relic is believed to have been left by a sailor from Granville or Régneville who once made a pilgrimage there. In the nearby town hall a 16-kg whale vertebra sits on top of a cupboard. It was entrusted to the mayor by an artist named Marc Petit after a trip to a community on the other side of the Atlantic with the same name, *La Baleine*.

As you leave the church, note Marie de Ballenoys' profession of faith from 1609 and take time out to dine at the Auberge du Krill, an inn named after a small shrimp devoured by the mastodons of the sea.

ATONEMENT AT CHAUSEY

Mass on the beach

50400 Granville
Typically organised on 15 August
Regular shuttles between Chausey and Granville

Wearing noble headgear to protect themselves from the sun, the islanders don't always don their Sunday best for Atonement Day. Casual wear is even advisable while listening to the sermon of Chausey priest Father Jean-Luc Lefrançois.

Once a year. on 15 August, the people of Chausey take time to gather and pray together. Far from the mainland, hymns resonate throughout the archipelago from morning till night. The morning celebration, often presided over by a bishop, isn't the only religious gathering of the day.

As night falls, a fervent aura envelops the procession of islanders. After casting a wreath in memory of those lost at sea, they leave the jetty and carry a statue of the Virgin Mary to their small chapel.

Quietly closing the doors behind them, they gather for a ceremony like no other, where the children's songs drown out the clinking of the masts of boats beached on the nearby shore.

Outside, nocturnal creatures take advantage of the calm to flutter happily under the celestial vault. It's a strange evening during which the islanders reach divine shores beyond the seas and Chausey's rocks. This religious event is an invitation to maritime tranquillity and island serenity.

Chausey blue lobster

While walking along the shores of all the islets in the Chausey archipelago at low tide, don't be surprised to encounter men and women carrying fishing gear. They're trying to find a rare gem: the Chausey lobster. These bluish-coloured crustaceans are renowned for their flavour. But they're becoming increasingly hard to find in the rocky crevices. On the other hand, fishing for *bouquet* (pink shrimp) remains a highly popular island pastime. These 'Chausey peanuts' are particularly enjoyed as an appetiser.

MATTHIEU ANGOT'S GARDEN

A miniature arboretum

Matthieu Angot
La Forge aux Balais
50320 Équilly
02 33 61 30 58
Access: departmental road Granville/Villedieu, direction Gavray, at Scion
junction, drive for 1.5 km to reach Angot's garage on the left

As a child Matthieu Angot collected reptiles and tarantulas. He still keeps some to this day. Now much taller, he has converted the scrapyard of his father's garage into a garden of exotic plants. Over an area of 2,000 square metres, surrounded by a bamboo hedge to the north and the garage to the south, he cultivates wild botanicals. In this astonishing microclimate you'll find pheasant berry shrubs, strawberry trees, tree ferns, eucalyptus, and a Japanese banana tree ...

These species from afar clearly thrive in this miniature arboretum, enhanced with shrubs and an impressive collection of succulents and

An unusual swamp pine waits to be discovered as you stroll around. Originating from Florida, it bears the longest needles of any tree in the world.

NEARBY
Logis d'Équilly

50320 Équilly
02 33 61 04 71
lelogisdequilly.fr

Logis d'Équilly is a former Norman manor just a stone's throw from Granville and Villedieu, in the Avranchin region. Built in the 13th century in Louis XIII style, it's now listed as a Historic Monument. In its 2-hectare lush green surroundings you'll discover an ancient tithe barn, a chapel and a dovecote. After the walk, why not indulge in regional local products in an 'empire' lounge.

Flower festival of La Haye-Pesnel

In 2016 the flower festival of La Haye-Pesnel, launched in 1953, celebrated its 23rd session. Every three years this event, which has been going for over 50 years, offers different themes such as operettas, famous films, literary masterpieces and renowned novels. The Haye-Pesnel residents, known as Haylands, create thousands of papillotes (decorative paper streamers) and attach them to huge floats. These parades through the streets of the town proudly represent the seven districts of the small community, including the centre, the fairground, the Thar river and the priory.

MILLENNIAL YEW
AT ÉGLISE DE LA BLOUTIÈRE

St Venice's witness

Église de La Bloutière
50800 La Bloutière
Church 16 km north-west of Villedieu

Standing at the entrance to the small communal cemetery of La Bloutière, the millennial yew tree is of unusual dimensions: over 12 metres tall and 8.3 metres in circumference.

As spring arrives the tree sometimes witnesses young women from the region passing by, on their way to pray to St Venice in the church.

According to local beliefs, St Venice is said to heal fertility issues and regulate menstrual flow. People express their wishes by leaving letters and red or blue ribbons, depending on the nature of their request. The multicoloured stone statue of the saint has been classified as a Historic Monument since 1975.

Other ancient yew trees in Normandy

According to the catalogue compiled by Henri Gadeau de Kerville in the late 19th century, Normandy is said to have 25 trees over a thousand years old. The oldest (1,500 to 1,600 years) could be the one in Mesnil-Ciboult (Manche department), which would be almost contemporaneous with those in Estry (Calvados), La Bloutière (Manche), Lande-Patry (Orne) and Haye-de-Routot (Eure). On the other hand, the ones in Saint-Ursin and Saint-Jean-le-Thomas, both in southern Manche, are noticeably younger. Incidentally, Celts living in non-Mediterranean Europe considered the yew as a symbol of immortality, death, and companion to those embarking on the afterlife.

For more on the yew tree and its symbolism, see p. 197.

NEARBY
Fountain for relieving liver disease   ㉛

La Fontaine de la Jaunisse
50800 Fleury

The community of Fleury, just a stone's throw from Villedieu, is home to one of the largest churches in southern Manche. Some parts of the building are believed to date back to the 14th century. A local fountain and oratory of Notre-Dame de la Jaunisse (Jaundice) are still visited by those with liver problems. At the site is an invitation to pilgrims to pray and have a Mass said. Devotion to Notre-Dame dates back to the 1880s. At that time, a parishioner from Villedieu church prayed by the fountain for the saint to heal her doctor husband. Legend says that the Virgin Mary appeared nearby as a statuette.

GREAT SACRAMENT OF THE ORDER OF MALTA

The Order of Malta at Villedieu-les-Poêles

Tourist office – 43 Place de la République
50800 Villedieu-les-Poêles-Rouffigny
02 33 61 05 69
Every four years, third Sunday after Pentecost

The small town of Villedieu-les-Poêles is perhaps the oldest French commandery founded by the Order of Malta (Knights Hospitallers religious military order). As early as 1187 it developed rapidly, welcoming pilgrims, the homeless and the sick, providing them with significant medical services 'without distinction of race or religion'. In this way it became a Vicus Dei (House of God), thanks to the generosity of benefactors and the commander. At the time the town was directly managed by the knights and residents paid no taxes. In memory of this glorious past, the people of Villedieu have hosted the Grand Sacre de l'Ordre (Great Sacrament of the Order) since the 15th century, on the third Sunday after Pentecost (interrupted during the French Revolution, resumed in 1955). In honour of the knights of Malta, they prepare a religious ceremony whose protocol is no less impressive than that of the British royal family. Six months before the festival the residents make garlands, decorations and banners to decorate the streets of their copper- and metal-working town. On the designated day a crowd gathers in this small Manche community of 4,000 people. There is a packed programme for everybody throughout a long day. In the morning, the knights of the Order sing the Veni Creator (Gregorian chant) at Notre-Dame church. Then the Holy Sacrament Mass is held in Parc de la Commanderie. In the afternoon, the knights of Malta parade, this time in procession and ceremonial attire,

in front of 7,000 to 10,000 spectators who respectfully line the route through Villedieu. At the front, the organisers are followed by children and a young shepherd representing St John the Baptist, the 'precursor' announcing the coming of the Messiah, accompanied by his lamb, the symbol of Sacrifice. Behind them walks the crowned Christ, embodied by a boy aged around 12. Then come the knights of Malta and the clergy, all dressed in black. Over three hours the procession stops at 10 temporary repositories – large altars set on a platform and embellished with a fresco.

Order of Malta: the privileges of its own country

The Sovereign Military Hospitaller Order of St John of Jerusalem of Rhodes and of Malta, commonly known as the Order of Malta, is one of the oldest Roman Catholic religious orders whose current mission is defence of the faith and assistance to the most vulnerable. Founded in Jerusalem around 1050 by merchants from the Italian Republic of Amalfi to assist pilgrims in the Holy Land, this monastic community dedicated to St John the Baptist was recognised as a religious order by Pope Paschal II in 1113.

The conquest of Jerusalem after the First Crusade in 1099 soon turned it into a military as well as a religious order, the second settle in the Holy Land after the Templars. After the loss of Jerusalem and Acre in 1291, the Order retreated to Cyprus from 1291 to 1309. Due to difficulties with the King of Cyprus, the Order conquered Rhodes, then under Byzantine rule, and made the island its new headquarters from 1310 until 1523. Insularity led to the Order developing a fleet that consolidated its reputation. Defeated by the Turks, the knights moved to Civitavecchia and then to Viterbo in Italy before going to Nice then settling in Malta in 1530. The island had been entrusted to them by Charles V, who understood its potential value against possible Ottoman advances. Napoleon expelled the Order from Malta in 1798, and it was eventually welcomed in Rome by the pope in 1834.

Before the loss of Malta, most members of the Order were clerics who had taken the three vows of poverty, chastity and obedience. Some members are still monks, but most of the knights and dames (11,000 nowadays) are laypersons. The military function has not been practised since 1798. Whereas past knights of the Order had to come from noble and chivalrous Christian families, it's now enough to distinguish yourself through faith, morality and merit towards the Church and the Order itself. While volunteers are always welcome, you can't apply to become a member.

The Order maintains diplomatic relations with 93 countries through its embassies. A very special status makes it the only private organisation to be treated almost like a separate country. Funding for its activities comes from the members themselves as well as private donations. In Rome, the Order has two headquarters that enjoy extraterritorial status: Palazzo Malta at No. 68 Via dei Condotti, where the Grand Master resides and the governing bodies meet, and Villa Malta in the Aventine neighbourhood, site of the Grand Priory of Rome, the Order's embassy to the Holy See and embassy to the Italian state.

Origin of the Maltese cross?

Founded in the mid-11th century in Jerusalem by Italian merchants, the Sovereign Military Hospitaller Order of St John of Jerusalem, known as the Order of Malta, adopted the emblem of the port of Amalfi, near Naples, but without retaining the blue background. In 1130, Raymond du Puy, who turned the charitable order into a military one, obtained from Pope Innocent II that their cross emblem should be white to differentiate it from the red cross of the Templars.

In 1523, expelled from the island of Rhodes by the Turks, the Order settled in Malta. The red flag of the island, inherited from the Norman occupation, then served as the backdrop for the white cross. The Maltese cross was born.

Significance of the eight points of the Maltese cross

The eight points of the Maltese cross have several meanings. They are said to represent:

- The eight sides of the Dome of the Rock in Jerusalem.
- The eight nationalities of the knights of the Order of St John of Jerusalem (the future Order of Malta) or the eight principles that these knights were expected to uphold: spirituality, simplicity, humility, compassion, justice, mercy, sincerity and patience.
- The virtues expected of the knights: loyalty, piety, frankness, courage, glory and honour, contempt for death, solidarity towards the poor and the sick, and respect for the Roman Catholic Church.

Note: For Christians, the points also symbolise the eight beatitudes exalted by Christ's Sermon on the Mount (according to St Matthew):

'Blessed are the poor in spirit, for theirs is the kingdom of heaven.' (Matt 5:3)

'Blessed are the meek, for they shall inherit the earth.' (Matt 5:5)

'Blessed are those who mourn, for they shall be comforted.' (Matt 5:4)

'Blessed are those who hunger and thirst for righteousness, for they shall be satisfied.' (Matt 5:6)

'Blessed are the merciful, for they shall receive mercy.' (Matt 5:7)

'Blessed are the pure in heart, for they shall see God.' (Matt 5:8)

'Blessed are the peacemakers, for they shall be called sons of God.' (Matt 5:9)

'Blessed are those who are persecuted for righteousness' sake, for theirs is the kingdom of heaven.' (Matt 5:12)

TORCHLIGHT STROLL IN VILLEDIEU-LES-POÊLES

The gentle cool of the evening

Night-time tour lasting 1¼ hr in Villedieu-les-Poêles
Departure from tourist office, every Fri 1 July–31 Aug, 8.30pm
Registration required until 7pm at tourist office:
43 Place de la République
02 33 61 05 69
Office hours: 9am–1pm & 1.30pm–7pm (in season)

Villedieu-les-Poêles. barely affected by the Second World War, is an old town built from undeniably attractive granite. It was the first commandery of the Hospitaller Order, and since the end of the Middle Ages, it has also been the headquarters of an unusual brotherhood of coppersmiths. The town is full of nooks and crannies, and the tourist office offers various ways to discover its 22 highlights. The most unusual option takes place in the coolness of the evening, by torchlight, in July and August.

You'll stroll through the steep, narrow streets of the quiet town accompanied by a guide, discovering its covered alleys and 35 courtyard-workshops where Maltese crosses are sometimes carved into the granite walls. You'll wander slowly from the district of the stone bridge to the historic heart of copper craftsmanship, passing by the grain market, the commandery park, the washhouses along the Sienne river, the Foyer, Bataille and Enfer (not to mention the Paradis) courtyards, the front of the bell foundry, and the Maison de l'Étain (Tin House).

Sourdins?

Far from being known as Villediens or Poêliens, as you might expect, Villedieu-les-Poêles residents are called 'Sourdins' (deaf), a term linked to the town's former activities of copper-smithing and pottery. The repeated hammering of copper eventually caused hearing loss, hence the name. It's perfect for a question-and-answer game with friends. Copper-smithing is the technique of shaping metals such as copper, brass, silver, or even tin, a craft that had its origins in the town of Dinant, Belgium.

Butterfly house

17 Rue du Docteur Havard
50800 Villedieu-les-Poêles-Rouffigny
If one little house catches the eye, it's at No. 17 Rue du Docteur Havard, in the town centre.
Here and there, the flower pots, meticulously maintained every day, coexist with large and magnificent multicoloured butterflies, elves, ladybugs ...
Over the years, this house has become an unusual attraction, repeatedly winning awards in various 'maisons fleuries' competitions in and around Villedieu-les-Poêles.

TOMB OF THE CORPORALS OF SOUAIN

34

Executed for refusal to obey in 1915 and rehabilitated in 1934 ...

Sartilly cemetery
50530 Sartilly-Baie-Bocage

A monument has stood in Sartilly cemetery since 1925 in memory of the four corporals from Souain (Marne) who were executed to set an example in 1915 and rehabilitated in 1934. Their names were Théophile Maupas, Lucien Lechat, Louis Girard and Louis Lefoulon.

All four of them were enlisted in the 6th battalion of the 336th infantry regiment from Saint-Lô during the First World War. On 9 March 1915 they were supposed to attack the Souain mill under a hail of German shells. However, their 21st company did not leave the trench. Tired and fatigued, the soldiers either didn't hear or didn't receive the order to attack. Outraged, their commander filed a complaint for refusal to obey. He refused to yield to his men and was determined to make examples at any cost.

On 16 March, 24 '*poilus*' ('hairy' French soldiers) stood before the military court in Suippes. At the end of the trial, 20 of them escaped a grim fate by successfully proving that the order hadn't been transmitted to them. However, the military jurisdiction showed no mercy towards the four corporals. They were sentenced to death for refusal to obey in the presence of the enemy. The following day, at 1pm in Châlons-sur-Marne, they were executed without being granted a reprieve, appeal, or right to clemency. Théophile Maupas (photo 1), born in Montgardon (Manche), 41 years old, was a schoolteacher and father of two children; Lucien Lechat (photo 2), born in Le Ferré (Ille-et-Vilaine), 24 years old, worked as a café waiter; Louis Girard (photo 3), born in Blainville (Manche), was a watchmaker and father of one child; Louis Lefoulon (photo 4), born in Calvados, 31 years old, was a father of one child.

Long after the war, Blanche Maupas, Théophile's widow, assisted by the League of Human Rights, made several appeals to have their judgement reviewed. Initially, on 16 March 1915, her efforts were rejected by the justice system. However, in 1934, following the publication of a book, her husband and his friends were rehabilitated by a special court of justice established in 1928 to review decisions of the military court. The magistrates were firm: the sacrifice demanded of them that day exceeded the limits of human endurance. In civilian life, they had impeccable conduct, and during the war they had shown their bravery in the face of the enemy. Several years later, the renowned filmmaker Stanley Kubrick drew inspiration from their story in his 1957 film *Paths of Glory*.

TROTTING RACES ON THE BEACH ㉟

Sandy hooves

Plage de Jullouville
50610 Jullouville
Once a year, in May, depending on tides

The charming seaside resort of Jullouville has organised horseraces on the beach every year since 1886. Between the shoreline and the waves, the equestrian world gathers for an extraordinary spectacle, almost unique in France. Only the commune of Plouescat in Brittany holds a similar event (see *Bretagne Nord insolite et secrète*, also published by Jonglez).

Far from traditional racecourses, members of the local equestrian society make it a point of honour to maintain this tradition on a few kilometres of sandy beach. Taking advantage of the ebbing tide (preferably after a high tide), they mark out a long track encircled by poles and ropes.

In exchange for a small entrance fee, the locals gather once a year in this vast equestrian and natural playground, aptly named '*hippodrome de la cale*' ('cove racetrack') for the occasion.

Horses from the Grand-Ouest (Brittany and Pays de la Loire) gallop swiftly along the shore, ridden by talented jockeys, to the delight of all spectators. 'Many of them train along the coast and appreciate this kind of terrain,' remarks a regular. As evening falls, the sea washes away all traces of galloping horses and spectators, erasing any evidence of their presence.

Above the beach the punters tally their winnings, street vendors count their cash and horse owners proudly display their trophies.

Horse races on the salt marshes of Mont-Saint-Michel

The south of Manche department is horse country. Idéal du Gazeau, hailing from Saint-Jean-le-Thomas, was a two-time winner of the Prix d'Amérique; and in Genêts horses and stables outnumber the locals.

Once a year, on the first Sunday of July, local residents create a full-scale racecourse from scratch. Grandstands, finish and starting posts are set up here and there on the meadows. In front of Mont-Saint-Michel, the trotting spectacle is always of high quality and contested by top jockeys.

NEARBY

Training grounds at Dragey dunes   ㊱

50530 Dragey-Ronthon

Dragey has also become a prominent location for racehorses. While waiting for a large training centre above the village, thoroughbreds and their jockeys speed along a natural track carved out of the dune ridge. In the early morning you can catch a glimpse of them ... but careful not to approach too closely. With Mont-Saint-Michel on the horizon, the spectacle is worth a visit. Just be sure not to spook the horses.

LOUIS-AUGUSTE ADRIAN'S TOMB

Adrian, father of the 'poilus' helmet

Genêts cemetery
50530 Genêts

During the winter of 1914 the '*poilus*' suffered heavy losses in trench warfare. Head injuries were the main cause of casualties. To protect the soldiers from shrapnel, quartermaster Louis Auguste Adrian (1859–1933) developed the M1915 helmet. From September 1915 over 7 million copies were distributed of this protective and lightweight steel headgear, inspired by the medieval *bourguignott* (burgonet) cavalry helmet. It was soon so successful that it was ordered en masse by French, Italian, Belgian, Serbian, Romanian, Russian and other military personnel.

The helmet, colour horizon blue, was affordable and made from relatively simple materials. The light steel weighed barely 700 grams. The effect was remarkable. By 1916, head injuries accounted for only 22 per cent of casualties. The grateful French Republic rewarded Adrian by promoting him to the rank of Commander of the Legion of Honour in October 1915. The quartermaster, saviour of hundreds of thousands of men, continued his work on protective armour throughout the First World War, developing body armour, armoured turrets for aviators, shrapnel-proof goggles, and more. He left the army in 1920 as a familiar figure to all. Married to the niece of the canon of Genêts, he later retired to his wife's hometown, where he passed away in 1933. His grave, a few metres from the war memorial at the entrance to the cemetery, is of course complete with an Adrian helmet.

His headgear was used by Serbian, Belgian, Romanian, Russian, Dutch and other police forces until the 1970s.

RETREAT
TO MONT-SAINT-MICHEL

Mont-Saint-Michel is also a spiritual site

Fraternité Monastique de Jérusalem
50170 Le Mont-Saint-Michel
02 33 58 31 71
info@abbaye-montsaintmichel.com
Hotels: Tues morning–Sun morning (stays limited to one week maximum)
Confirm 48 hours in advance by mail or phone

Since 2001, the Monastic Brotherhood of Jerusalem has welcomed those wishing to make a spiritual retreat at Mont-Saint-Michel. Apart from the interest of retiring from the world for a few days, the retreat is also an opportunity to discover the Mount in a special way. Prayers, vigils and processions are regularly held in the abbey itself, after the doors close. Gathered quietly in one of Christianity's most beautiful buildings, you can avoid the hordes of tourists who flock there during the day.

On some celebratory occasions, doors usually closed to visitors are opened to retreatants. But with certain exceptions the retreat requires that both monastic communities comply with silent prayer at 6.30am, Lectio divina from 8.30am to 9.30am, Eucharist at 12.15pm, Adoration of Holy Sacrament at 4.30pm, Vespers at 6.30pm and Compline at 8.30pm.

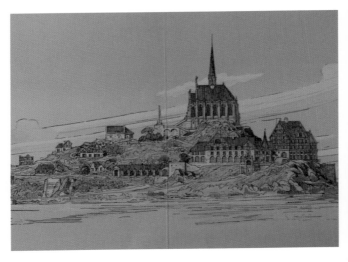

The brethren and sisters sometimes ask people to take part in community work during their stay. Most rooms (single or double) are in Mont-Saint-Michel houses, although there are some within the abbey. Meals are taken in silence (men and women separately) and in fine weather coffee is even served on a small private terrace, spectacularly overlooking the Mount.

Fraternités Monastiques de Jérusalem

The Monastic Fraternities of Jerusalem bring together those whose vocation is to create oases of prayer, silence and peace in town. They were established on All Saints' Day 1975 in the church of Saint-Gervais-Saint-Protais, Paris, at the wishes of Cardinal François Marty and Father Pierre-Marie Delfieux, student chaplain at the Sorbonne and founder of the Fraternitiés de Jérusalem. They are now based in Paris, Vézelay, Strasbourg, Mont-Saint-Michel, Brussels, Florence, Montreal and Rome (see *Secret Rome*, also published by Jonglez) – as well as two places of reception and retreat: Magdala in Sologne (central France) and Gamogna in Tuscany. Monks and nuns, always dressed in blue, replaced the Benedictine monks at Mont-Saint-Michel in 2001.

When Tombelaine almost became a casino

The islet of Tombelaine (or the legendary Helen's tomb) lies in the bay of Mont-Saint-Michel. At the beginning of the 20th century it was coveted by a rather extravagant developer. On behalf of the Groupement International de la Baie du Mont-Saint-Michel, Georges Anquetil planned to build from scratch a casino, a luxury hotel, hanging gardens, ramparts and a church with a bell tower as imposing as that of the 13th-century Gothic part of the abbey, known as La Merveille (The Wonder). Fortunately, the project derailed and Tombelaine, saved from the folly of grandeur, was taken over by the state in 1933. The small island is now an ornithological reserve, inhabited by gulls, egrets … sometimes disturbed by ramblers around the bay and guides helping them to avoid the notorious quicksands.

SUSPENSION BRIDGE OF ÉGLISE DE DUCEY

An unfinished church

50220 Ducey-les-Chéris

Yes, it's true. From a distance, the astonishing Saint-Pair-de-Ducey church looks unfinished. Up close, even more so. The building is divided into two and only connected by a small bridge, sometimes used by carpenters. Between the two sections is empty space. The reason is simple: the choir and nave were built in the late 19th century under the guidance of Canon Gourdel to the plans of architect Nicolas Théberge, replacing an older construction from the 18th century. Due to lack of funds, the two planned towers topped with bells were never built. They had to settle for the old bell tower a few metres away, dating from 1828 and fortunately not destroyed by the prudent priest.

To see the final form that Ducey church would have had if completed, you'll need to travel a few kilometres to Sartilly. In this commune between Granville and Avranches, a church was indeed completed according to Théberge's plans.

NEARBY
Oldest bridge in Manche

Ducey is a charming little flowery commune on the banks of the Sélune river, crossed by the oldest bridge in the region, built in 1613. The date is engraved on the parapet.

The bridge, listed on the supplementary inventory of Historic Monuments of France, was used by pilgrims and merchants travelling to Mont-Saint-Michel. Delicate restoration work has recently been undertaken on the bridge by Manche department.

Baptistery of Saint-Hilaire-du-Harcouët (41)
Place de l'église
50600 Saint-Hilaire-du-Harcouët

The venerable tower of the former church of Saint-Hilaire-du-Harcouët was erected by the Benedictine nuns of Laumondais priory. The tower, designated a Historic Monument in 1921, is remarkable for its corner buttresses, pointed arch windows, and frescoes by Marthe Flandrin. The frescoes date from 1947 when the building was solemnly consecrated as a baptistery by the Manche bishop. Baptisms are still occasionally celebrated by the parish priest.

STEPHEN BOSCHER, THATCHER

Passion for old thatched houses

50150 Sourdeval-la-Barre
Open Thurs in July and Aug (organised by Chamber of Commerce)
02 33 90 13 02

While there are barely 70 thatchers in the whole of France, Stephen Boscher is the only one in Manche department who builds thatched cottages. This profession was surely meant for him, as he was born in one such cottage, owned by his parents.

When his childhood home was being restored by a skilled craftsman, he didn't miss a single step. Remembering his time in the thatched cottage, he reconnected with the thatcher when deciding on a career after his national service. He now works independently, armed only with a clamp, trowel, pair of scissors, sawhorse and roll of wire, tirelessly working on houses with thatched roofs.

Those close to him say that his order book is full for years to come,

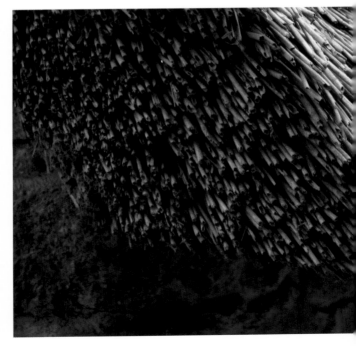

as he's gained experience and skills since his early days in the Pays d'Auge, not far from Deauville. The construction of such a thatched roof is much more time-consuming and expensive than a slate roof, but its lifespan (40 years), low maintenance and exceptional thermal and acoustic insulation make it a worthwhile investment.

NEARBY
Eucharistic casket from the 7th century (43)
Église Saint-Evroult, 50140 Mortain-Bocage

The dark sandstone church of Saint-Evroult stands austerely in the centre of Mortain. Behind a Romanesque door with typical Norman geometric decoration, the treasury room houses a rare Eucharistic casket. This precious object was used to transport the Eucharist during ceremonies. Known as the Chrismale, it dates from the 7th century and bears figures of Christ Pantocrator, St Michael and St Gabriel, with an Anglo-Saxon inscription. Also worth seeing is the illuminated Gospel, probably drawn up by an English scriptorium in the 10th century.

PARISIAN STREET SIGNS IN NOTRE-DAME-DU-TOUCHET VILLAGE

Paris in the countryside

50140 Notre-Dame-du-Touchet (commune of Mortain-Bocage)
Between Mortain and Saint-Hilaire via D977 and then D46; in south-east of
department

Notre-Dame-du-Touchet in the southern Manche region was once home to a mischievous junk dealer. In the 1980s, he acquired a stock of old Parisian street signs and had the eccentric idea of fixing them here and there around his village. With the approval of the then mayor, Claude Lebigot, cast iron and enamel plaques began to appear at every corner. Today only one is missing: Avenue du Général de Gaulle. One night somebody took it away for a joke. But the other 60 signs are still untouched, much to the dismay of postal and telecommunications workers.

Wander along Boulevard de la Chapelle and Rue de Varenne, right in the middle of the village. Take time to discover Place de la Pucelle, Rond-Point des Champs-Élysées and Rue de l'Égalité, leading to the communal cemetery. In this extraordinary journey through Paris, you'll also come across signage for the Porte de Vanves metro station on the former D84 departmental road.

With a little imagination this leads you to the village bistro at the corner of Avenue des Ternes and the bakery on Rue de Suresnes. While

enjoying *teurgoule* (a local dessert made with rice, milk and cinnamon), don't forget to pass by Place de la République, Avenue Foch, Passage des Épinettes and … Avenue Patton. During the D-Day landings of the Second World War, a stopover by the famous American general is still remembered by Notre-Dame-du-Touchet residents.

The junk dealer obtained his stock from a former Parisian scrap dealer at a time when the cast iron and enamel signs were being replaced with plastic inscriptions.

LA FOSSE ARTHOUR

Legend of King Arthur

50720 Saint-Georges de Rouelley

La Fosse Arthour (Arthur's Cavern) is a gorge 70 metres deep where a torrent flows through rocks worn by time. Legend has it that a foliage-covered cave is hidden within one of the cliffs. It's known as the chambre de la reine (queen's chamber). Another rocky cavity on the opposite bank is named the chambre du roi (king's chamber), said to be in memory of the hero of the Round Table, Arthur, King of the two Britains.

Arthur frequented these places along with his beloved companion Guinevere, who he was forbidden from courting until sunset. But, overwhelmed by love, he broke the pact that bound him to a faerie before the sun had set.

Punishment struck without delay: he was engulfed body and soul in the little river, swollen by the heavenly powers. Seeing her lover swallowed by the infernal waters, Guinevere had no wish to survive him. She threw herself off a cliff and joined him in the abyss.

Locals have claimed ever since that two crows as white as swans were wont to glide gently above the torrent. The birds, protected by local farmers, would drive away predators from the sky. But one evening they flew beyond the horizon and were never seen again.

Others tell the tale that farmers used to toss a coin into the torrent. Not without reason: they knew that the following day, two black bulls would emerge from the water to help them with their ploughing. But once evening fell the animals had to be brought back to Fosse Arthour with a bundle of hay tied to their horns, so they could plunge back into their watery home in the best possible way.

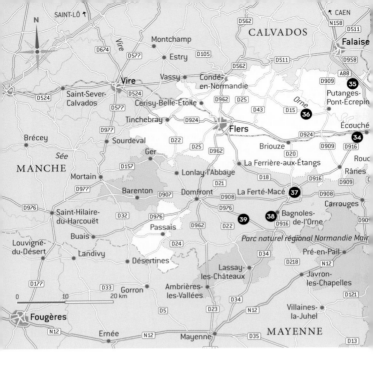

Orne

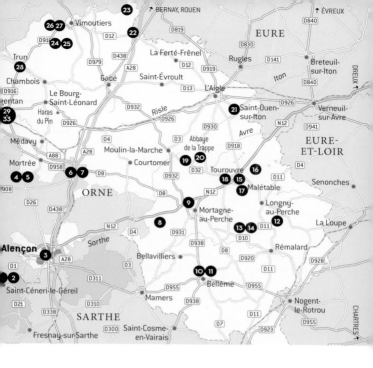

BEES' NEST AT ÉGLISE PROTECTIVE BEES

 ①

Bienen als Beschützerinnen

61250 Saint-Céneri-le-Géreil

The origin of the curious hole in the left back wall of Saint-Céneri-le-Géreil church is explained by a small sign.

In 898 Charles the Simple (Charles III of France) sent his army to the village to fight the Normans. The legend goes that the soldiers were behaving disrespectfully near the church that housed the tomb of St Céneri (Benedictine monk Serenicus, an early evangelist in Normandy). As a punishment they were attacked by bees.

The panicking soldiers didn't know where to flee. In their confusion they ended up throwing themselves off the cliff and into the Sarthe river. Most of them drowned, weighed down by their armour.

Since then there's been a bees' nest in the wall of the village church, still looked after by local beekeepers.

ST SERENICUS' BED

Curing incontinence and infertility

Chapelle de Saint-Céneri
61250 Saint-Céneri-le-Gérei
June–Sept (ask at town hall beforehand)
At foot of church

Just a few steps from the church, a small chapel stands in a green meadow overlooking the river. This chapel is believed to have been built in the 15th century on the site of St Serenicus' hermitage (he died in 670). Inside, a slab of granite is known as the hermit's bed.

Two traditions are associated with the stone: children suffering from incontinence would lie on it to be cured, and women would go to sleep on it to boost their chances of pregnancy.

For many centuries the place was also frequented by young girls in search of a husband. To declare their wish they would jab a needle into the statue's feet. If the needle stuck, they were supposed to find a partner within the year.

BALCONIES OF ALENÇON

Balconies like no others

61000 Alençon
Fact sheet on balconies at Alençon tourist office,
Maison d'Ozé, Place de la Madgeleine: 02 33 80 66 33

In the early 20th century local scholars identified 170 wrought-iron balconies from the Louis XV era and 75 from the Louis XVI era in Alençon town centre.

Without the success of the royal lace factories, printers and publishers, the people of Alençon probably wouldn't have built their richly ornate private mansions.

These unique balconies can be seen by everyone as they are always built on the 'noble' first floor of beautiful residences. Look up as you walk along Grande-Rue, as well as Rue du Jeudi (an example at No. 63), Rue du Bercail (at No. 23), Rue du Cygne, Rue des Marcheries and Rue des Grandes Porteries ...

These architectural features, which can be spotted on a leisurely stroll between Cours Clemenceau and the grain market, are sometimes so finely crafted that you can't help but think of lace-making. The only obvious difference is the material used. These balconies are the work of

skilled ironworkers who used ore extracted from the region's mines and processed in nearby forges.

At No. 16 Rue du Château, a scallop shell is carved below a wrought-iron balcony. This is believed to be a symbol indicating the right track for pilgrims heading to Santiago de Compostela.

'Whosoever lifts me, Alençon will perish!'

At No. 2 Rue du Château, the Café des Sept Colonnes (open weekdays only) is a curious two-storey building dating from the 15th century. It has red timber framing, a peculiar gable and uneven windows. The story goes that its cellar vault was supported by a pillar that, if it collapsed, would cause the town to flood. Others suggested that the underground chamber contained a slab that should never be moved.

'Whosoever lifts me, Alençon will perish!' was the terrible proclamation. Alençon residents with their taste for the supernatural firmly believed in this story, but the simple explanation could be the existence of an underground canal that brought water from the Sarthe river to the vault, probably passing beneath Café des Sept Colonnes.

FORGIVENESS FOR MOTORISTS

Have your car blessed

Place de l'Église
61570 Saint-Christophe-le-Jajolet (commune of Boischampré)
Last Sunday July and first Sunday Oct

S t Christopher is the patron saint of motorists and travellers 'on land, at sea, and in the air'. Numerous churches, sanctuaries and municipalities throughout France bear his name. The parish of Saint-Christophe-le-Jajolet is one of them.

This church is possibly the oldest, with manuscripts dating back to the year 1000 attesting to its existence. In 1911 the parish priest organised the first pilgrimage for motorists there, with the blessing of Pope Pius X. This event now takes place on the last Sunday of July and the first Sunday of October in the church square, in the shade of lime trees near a statue of the patron saint. Each year you can witness the blessing of beautiful bodywork in the presence of proud car owners – a most unusual sight.

St Christopher and the Golden Legend

According to legend it was St Christopher who carried the Christ child on his shoulders to help him cross a torrent. The Greek origin of his name is revealing: *Christos – phoros*, meaning 'the one who carries Christ'.

The story of the saint was recounted by Jacobus de Voragine, a Genoese Dominican friar from the 14th century. He compiled his narratives in the *Golden Legend*. This text is one of the major works of Christianity, recounting the lives of 180 saints, martyrs and Christian figures, as well as certain episodes from the life of Christ. All accounts follow the liturgical calendar.

According to his description, Christopher was a giant who lived in the 3rd century CE and worked as a ferryman. While searching for a powerful person to serve, one day he ferried a child across the river. As the weight in the boat increased, he realised that the child was none other than Christ himself who, because of the sins of the world he carried on his shoulders, threatened to sink the boat. Christopher immediately converted to Christianity.

As there wasn't enough historical evidence for his actual existence, St Christopher was removed from the calendar of saints in 1970. Prior to that he had been, among other things, the patron saint of travellers. Still, numerous relics are attributed to him: a tooth in Rome, an arm in Santiago de Compostela, a rib in Venice, some bones in Braga (Portugal) and Tuscany (Italy), and his head on Rab island (Croatia).

NEARBY

Château de Sassy ⑤

61200 Saint-Christophe-le-Jajolet (commune of Boischampré)
02 33 35 32 66
Check website for opening hours and days: chateaudesassy.fr
The superb Sassy castle houses a wealth of furniture and royal tapestries. Interesting guided tours are available.

SCULPTURE OF
THE *BEAU DIEU DE SÉEZ*

The last work of Bernini

Cathédrale de Sées
61500 Sées

⑥

The sculpture known as the *Beau Dieu de Séez*, a magnificent work in white Carrara marble. stands in the south transept of Sées cathedral (sometimes spelled Séez). Few know that it was authenticated in 1999 as the last major work of Bernini, the Italian master sculptor and architect, carved in Rome in 1678 for Queen Christina of Sweden. The bust was offered to the cathedral around 1780 by Bishop du Plessis d'Argentré (1775–1801), bishop of the Diocese of Sées and a benefactor of the town and its cathedral. Note that the sculpture is often loaned to exhibitions around the world.

NEARBY
Lifting wheel of the cathedral   ⑦
Cathédrale de Sées
61500 Sées
Visits during Heritage Days

To build cathedrals, medieval workers used two lifting methods: winch and wheel. While the winch was used on the ground, the wheel was used in the upper structures. In 1979, the Art et Cathédrale association restored a wheel 28 metres above the ground, directly over the west portal in the extension of the vaults. Someone walking in this wheel could lift about 12 times their own weight, so if a man weighed 80 kg he could hoist nearly one tonne.

Florence cathedral also has a relic of the winch that was used on the facade to raise the heaviest stones to the top (see *Secret Florence* and *Secret Tuscany*, both published by Jonglez).

ÉGLISE SAINT-AUBIN AT BOËCÉ

A church moved by sheer willpower!

61560 Boëcé

According to an old legend, in 1764 the residents of Boëcé (a commune between Le Mêle-sur-Sarthe and Mortagne-au-Perche) moved their church using only the sheer strength of their arms together with their faith.

That year a square tower was being built in Boëcé village. The construction work was clearly unwelcome. People feared that the excavation machinery would damage the church as it passed. To avoid such a disaster, they all met one Sunday afternoon after vespers. From peasants to carpenters and bakers, everyone was there. Equipped with thick hemp ropes, they formed two groups and each pulled one side, guided by the priest and the sexton. Their hard work eventually paid off – the church had moved back a few centimetres. The evidence was plain to see on the damp ground ...

While many locals have never believed such a story, everyone in Boëcé is adamant that it's true, even today. A commemorative Mass is celebrated in the church once a year, on the weekend of 1 May.

© Ch bougui

FOIRE AUX BOUDINS

Blood sausage in all its variations

61400 Mortagne-au-Perche
Once a year, in March

The Mortagne-au-Perche Blood Sausage Fair takes place once a year, usually in the month of March.

Revived in the 1950s by the local tourist office, the fair sells 6 to 7 tonnes of this regional product during three days of festivities. Since March 1963 its success has been growing thanks to the Confrérie des Chevaliers du Goûte Boudin (Brotherhood of Blood Sausage Tasters). Always looking for fresh ideas, members hold a competition for the best sausage that attracts hundreds of French and European producers (from Austria, Italy, Spain and Germany) every year.

Each time, the special sausage is served in various ways, accompanied by cheese, prunes, raisins, and sometimes even fish, scallops or other seafood.

The biggest blood sausage-eating contest

The highlight of the Blood Sausage Fair is undoubtedly the contest for the champion sausage eater. In front of nearly 3,000 spectators, competitors try to swallow as much as possible, with the record to beat around 2.5 kg in 15 minutes.

Cooking blood sausage follows a long-standing tradition in the Perche region. The chosen date for this operation is mid-Lent, which coincides with a fair that took place at that time in the Middle Ages.

An original recipe: tripe skewers

Boucherie Le Goff
31 Rue Saint-Denis
61600 La Ferté-Macé
02 33 37 11 85

Le Goff butcher's shop is known for its tripe skewers. They are made exclusively in La Ferté-Macé but sold all around France and the rest of Europe.

The recipe is said to have been invented by a couple of loggers. They cooked beef tripe from a butcher in a pot with butter and Calvados brandy. This was so successful that they opened a restaurant. Faced with the appetite of some greedy customers who left nothing for others, they devised a clever trick – they packaged their tripe in portions, skewering the pieces of meat together.

STATUE OF A YOUNG GIRL PLAYING 'COLIN-MAILLARD'

Origin of 'blind man's buff'?

28 Rue Ville Close – 61130 Bellême

Opposite Bansard-des-Bois hotel in the town of Bellême, passers-by might notice a strange statue of a young girl playing '*colin-maillard*' ('blind man's buff'). The work, by Victor-Edmond Leharivel-Durocher from Orne, was offered to the town by art connoisseur Marquis de Chennevières in the 19th century. The aim was to mock the

blindness of the residents, who had refused the coming of the railway along with the progress it would bring.

The origins of the game aren't widely known, but it involves one blindfolded player trying to catch and identify others. The French name may come from Jean Colin-Maillard, a warrior who fought the Count of Louvain in the 10th century. He's said to have added the name 'Maillard' to his own because of the formidable mallet he wielded.

Despite having his eyes gouged out in battle, he continued to fight by randomly striking around him with his preferred weapon, the mallet.

A face with dead eyes is also represented on a stone carving of the portrait of Johan Coley Maillard, known as 'Le Grand Maillard' and his wife Jeanne de Seille. This can be seen on one of the monumental chimneys of the old Château de Landreville in Ardennes, his family's ancestral home.

NEARBY

Photograph by Nadar in Mairie de Bellême ⑪

Beside two wooden cages where criminals used to be confined, the town-hall meeting room is home to an 'aerostatic' photograph by the famous Nadar, French photographer and balloonist. As its name suggests, the shot was taken from a hot-air balloon. It shows a partial view of Bellême, taken at an altitude of 1,100 metres, at 4.40 on a July morning in 1886.

Mycologiades Internationales de Bellême

The International Mycologiades of Bellême have been bringing together mushroom specialists from around the world since 1953. This major gathering takes place over five days, usually on the last weekend of September or the first weekend of October. The Mycologiades offer exhibitions, meetings, lectures, drawing contests, discovery workshops and, of course, outings to learn how to identify fungi. These events, which bring together professionals and enthusiasts, cover a wide range of topics including health, cuisine, the environment, and more. In addition to a professional mycology test open to pharmacists and assistants, a golden cep is awarded to the best picker among the younger participants. The mycological walks take place in the beautiful forest of Bellême, long renowned for its fungi.

WEATHER-VANE MAKER
THIERRY SORET

Wind and weather vanes

Le Bourg – 61290 Le Mage
02 33 73 62 60
Visits by appointment only

Rural people often kept a weather vane at the bottom of their garden or on the roof of their house. And they still decorate the roofs of churches and the homes of those who prefer the precise science of their oscillations to the weather forecast.

In a small village at the heart of Le Perche region, one of the few remaining weather-vane and sign-makers in France carries out his work. Since a very young age Thierry Soret dreamed of creating these astonishing little wind machines, as he watched the one on his grandfather's house. Since 1993, as a trained artist and craftsman in drawing and metalwork, he's been self-employed. His main job is to craft custom-made and personalised weather vanes to his customers' requirements.

Using copper for the framework and brass for the scenes and compass roses, this artisan works up to 12 hours on each piece to create his beautiful artworks. Whether simple or intricate, they transport us far into our own dreams or even back in time, offering up to 400 different scenes: a peasant ploughing the field, the French rooster, the clockmaker, the doctor, the deer hunt ...

History of the weather vane

The oldest known weather vane, the Tower of the Winds in Athens, with its bronze triton celebrating the wind, is said to have been designed by a Syrian architect and astronomer between the 2nd and 1st centuries BCE. A little later, in the 8th century, they were used on Viking longships to gauge the strength of the winds and as protection from the wind gods. But only in the Middle Ages did weather vanes become a symbol of the power of Church and nobility. Instead of being fixed on their axis, they went mobile with Leonardo da Vinci, who himself invented the first meteorological instrument. During the French Revolution the vanes descended from church steeples to grace the homes of ordinary people. They were widely offered as wedding gifts or made into signs for blacksmiths, butchers or bakers. They enjoyed their heyday for several centuries until the arrival of radio and television weather bulletins. Disappearing from rooftops, they are now conserved in certain museums, such as Rouen's Musée Le Secq des Tournelles, devoted to the art of wrought ironwork. Some of these vanes can reach 1.8 metres in height.

PONTGIRARD GARDENS

13

The elegance of a garden

Manoir du Pontgirard
61290 Monceaux-au-Perche (commune of Longny-les-Villages)
02 33 73 61 49
1 May–30 Sept, 2.30pm–6.30pm, Sat, Sun and public holidays
Outside opening days and hours, go to manor porch

Pontgirard manor, standing at the foot of the Jambée stream, is still a beautiful building. Built in the mid-16th century by a family of ironsmiths, the dwelling was renovated the following century during the reign of Louis XIV.

In 1994 owner Philippe Siguret entrusted landscape gardener Thierry Hay with the task of creating a flower garden. These terraced gardens, not far from Réno-Valdieu forest and now listed as Historic Monuments, rival the green landscapes of Le Perche. Since 1997 they've been open to the public.

Far from the town, the various pathways with their wells, ash trees, oaks and dogwood lead visitors to welcoming pergolas and refreshing fountains. Here and there, collections of euphorbia, a two-hundred-year-old lime tree, an orchard, a pond, hydrangeas, irises and aromatic plants are an open invitation to discover harmonious colours and a range of scents. During the summer season, themed visits are organised for interested parties.

NEARBY
Monceaux-au-Perche village

14

Monceaux-au-Perche, a few kilometres from Mortagne-au-Perche and south-east of Réno-Valdieu forest, lies at the confluence of two streams, the Commeauche and the Jambée. Like Longny-au-Perche, Ceton and La Perrière, this picturesque village typical of the region is the site of two charming manors built in the 16th century. This model of harmony is worth a visit for its single street lined with houses with brown and red tiled roofs, and its ochre facades. The church dedicated to St John the Baptist, encircled by a quaint cemetery, has preserved a remarkable Romanesque gateway.

ÉGLISE D'AUTHEUIL

Such a grand church for such a small village

61190 Autheuil (commune of Tourouvre-au-Perche)

A huge surprise on arriving from the main road – the church of Autheuil, overlooking a field where cows graze peacefully, dominates the horizon. What is such a grand religious building doing in such a small community? While many explanations have been given by locals and historians over the centuries, it's difficult to settle on one, although it is highly likely that this monumentality is due to the former presence of a Templar commandery.

This lovely church is in Romanesque style except for two windows on the south side, one dating back to the 16th century and the other flamboyant Gothic. Classified as a Historic Monument since 1875, the church was built in the early 12th century. It was dependent on the nearby Abbaye de Saint-Évroult, which appointed its priests and collected tithes.

Today's historians have very little documentation on the church construction. But rather more is known about the facade, which was entirely rebuilt by V. Ruprich Robert, a student of Viollet-le-Duc. He left his mark by installing an Irish-style cross at the very top, which was mistaken for three skulls by 19th-century congregations ...

© GO69

Promoter of Percheron exports to Canada

In the nave of Autheuil church, a large plaque is placed in memory of Robert Giffard, Sieur de Mancel. Born in Autheuil around 1590, he was the promoter of Percheron draught horse exports to Canada and a pioneer of New France.

CHAUFFETIÈRES BRICKWORKS

Ancestral know-how

Monsieur and Madame Fontaine
61290 L'Hôme-Chamondot
02 33 83 39 26
Can be visited during Heritage Days

In the last century there were 32 kilns in Orne department producing tiles and bricks. The Fontaine family of L'Hôme-Chamondot has perpetuated this ancestral know-how for four generations. There were Auguste, Georges, Hubert and now Laurent.

From childhood, the men get their hands dirty and discover a trade that draws upon earth, water, air and fire, these four fundamental elements. Every year, three batches of bricks are handmade using the naturally occurring soil beneath Charency woods, rich in sand and iron, giving them their distinctive colour.

The freezing temperatures of winter slow down the pace of work. But as soon as mid-April arrives the brickworks spring back to life. The moisture added to the clay is judged by eye, without meticulous measurements. Then the wooden molds are filled shortly before turning them out again for quick drying.

Two or three days later, the brick adventure continues with a two-month drying period under cover, followed by a passage through the Gallo-Roman kiln. These bricks are used for historic monuments such as Château de Carrouges and Versailles Palace, as well as old residences. Their smooth edges and even their imperfections contribute to an enduring aesthetic appeal.

The bricks were originally made at a place called Les Chauffetières. It was rebuilt for practical reasons at the beginning of the 20th century but is still flanked by two large buildings, the first dating back to 1760 and the second to 1875. Both are listed as Historic Monuments.

© Nathalie Fontaine

NOTRE-DAME DE LA SALETTE CHURCH TOWER

An extravagant extension

61290 Malétable (commune of Longny-les-Villages)
02 33 25 61 30
Visits only on third Sun of June, July, Aug, Sept and during Heritage Days
Free of charge

© Unozoe

É glise de Notre-Dame de La Salette was constructed under the guidance of Abbot Migorel in the second half of the 19th century. The church is worth visiting for its whimsical eclectic style, decorated with glazed bricks, and its octagonal tower built between 1866 and 1872 and restored in 1980.

Visitors can't fail to miss the stained-glass window at the top of the peculiar neo-Baroque bell tower that lights up at nightfall. It houses the Virgin Mary, accompanied by Maximin and Mélanie, the two young Dauphinois to whom she appeared in 1846.

Three of the church turrets are crowned with archangels Raphael and Gabriel in cast iron, and Michael in terracotta, while the fourth has always been empty.

The church was opened for worship in 1866 and consecrated on 11 October by Monseigneur Rousselet, Bishop of Sées.

Apparition of La Salette

On 19 September 1846 two children, Maximin Giraud (age 11) and Mélanie Calvat (age 14), encounter a 'beautiful lady' in the Alpine meadows above the village of La Salette in south-eastern France (Dauphiné). The Virgin Mary, sitting down in tears, speaks at length with them in French and the local dialect. Before leaving she imparts a message, instructing them to spread it to 'all her people'. Then she climbs up a path and disappears into the light.

Two years later, on the same date, Monseigneur Philibert de Bruillard, Bishop of Grenoble, recognised the apparition. 'It bears within itself all the characteristics of truth,' he proclaimed in a famous decree. 'The faithful are justified in believing it indubitable and certain.' Abbot Migorel, deeply affected by the phenomenon, wished to pay homage to the Virgin.

Abbot's dream

As a curate in Laleu in 1857, Abbot Jules-Clément Migorel, born in 1826, had a vision in one of his dreams of a church built on a hilltop. The dream would become reality in Malétable a few years later. Appointed in 1863 to this small commune in Orne, he mobilised donations and bequests in order to build Notre-Dame de la Salette. Abbot Migorel spent more than 26 years in Malétable. He retired to La Ferté-Macé, where he died in 1904.

MUSÉE DE COMMERCES ET MARQUES

'Here, everyone found something'

Muséales de Tourouvre
Rue Mondrel
61190 Tourouvre-au-Perche
02 33 83 30 64

Pierre Marzorati, formerly in the retail trade, has always been an enthusiast for the commerce of yesteryear. His collection spans the years 1900 to the 1960s. Over the course of some 20 years he acquired over 20,000 artefacts on his professional travels. Venturing off the beaten path, he enjoyed pushing open the creaky door of an antiquarian to find a Banania tin, advertising fans, old electric razors, vintage hairdryers, spools of thread. Long before others, Marzorati had assembled an unusual bric-a-brac of objects, highly sought after today by cool collectors. But what did he mean to do with it?

In Lignerolles, the small village where he lives, he set up a trades museum in 1988. With a smile he invited visitors to follow him into a sort of Ali Baba's cave filled with a thousand forgotten treasures. Following the guide, you enter an original hairdresser's salon, a grocery store, a dairy shop, a bar, a toy store, an apothecary. In all he recreated a dozen commercial outlets where visitors could finger enamel signs,

metal boxes lined up on wooden shelves. In this peculiarly baroque place, visitors would rediscover their childhood, encountering old customs and traditions and sometimes even the scents of the past. 'Here, everyone found something,' explains the collector.

To make sure that his efforts would be preserved, Marzorati sought a successor. He didn't have to look far. The Tourouvre community near Mortagne-au-Perche acquired the valuable collection. It offers a journey into the commerce of the past, through the exploration of iconic brands.

NEARBY

Soligny-la-Trappe village

A few km from Tourouvre and 12 km north of Mortagne
61475 Soligny-la-Trappe

Soligny-la-Trappe, a short distance from the Trappist monastery Abbaye de La Grande Trappe, is a charming, flower-filled village. Its church, Saint-Germain d'Auxerre (late 11th century), features a Romanesque portal topped with a chevron frieze. From the cemetery you can enjoy a beautiful view of the lushly wooded Perche countryside.

Rancé oak tree (20)

On road facing La Trappe abbey, 10-min walk from sign on right

The oak, named after the abbot who made La Trappe abbey famous, is over 300 years old. With a circumference of 4.3 metres and a crack in the trunk 3.2 metres long, it has endured the ravages of time and storms. It's said that President François Mitterrand once paid discreet homage to the tree.

CHIMNEYS OF SAINT-OUEN-SUR-ITON VILLAGE

Spiral chimneys

61300 Saint-Ouen-sur-Iton
6 km south-east of L'Aigle

The Église de Saint-Ouen-sur-Iton was once surrounded only by a presbytery and a farm. It's now in the heart of a village with over 800 residents, built by former mayor Désiré Guillemare, starting in 1871 and officially inaugurated on 27 August 1898. But not many tourist brochures invite visitors to explore this small Orne commune.

Yet this village 6 km south-east of L'Aigle is a curiosity with its unusual houses and twisted spiral chimneys. From simple shops to bourgeois villas, from bakery to town hall, almost every building has its brick extension reaching towards the Normandy skies.

Guillemare, a wealthy farmer who served as mayor of the commune for many years, had this whimsical idea in the 19th century, hoping that his village would be remembered for generations to come. He didn't hesitate to spend a fortune to accomplish his life's work.

Désiré Guillemare, a megalomaniac benefactor

In 1899 Désiré Guillemare, mayor of Saint-Ouen-sur-Iton, made a generous gift to the village. He donated a massive bell weighing 47.5 kg on condition that it would chime every hour and be rung for both rich and poor burials. He also undertook various construction projects in the village, including bridges, the old town hall, school, post office and telegraph office, theatre and covered market. In a touch of megalomania, he erected a 14-metre-high pyramid-shaped column in the main square of the village, dedicated to his own glory. Crowned with a small statue, the column bears cast-iron plaques telling of the deeds and actions of the philanthropic mayor. As another gesture, Guillemare once provided the young children of the village with caps so they could raise them to greet the villagers and, of course, himself. The benefactor passed away in 1904 and was buried in the cemetery, where his grave is easily recognisable among all the others. Anything less would have been surprising.

Grants for twisted chimneys!

Today, residents who want to erect a twisted chimney on their roof can do so ... and claim a subsidy from the town hall.

FORGOTTEN VILLAGE OF LE SAP

A charming village off the beaten track

Border of Pays d'Auge and Pays d'Ouche
Syndicat d'Initiative (tourist office)
61470 Le Sap (commune of Sap-en-Auge)

The picturesque village of Le Sap is full of character. This small and charming commune, a curiosity in itself, is classified as a protected area for architectural, urban and landscape heritage. On the border of Pays d'Auge and Pays d'Ouche, the village is worth a visit for the typical narrow streets, gilded facades, small courtyards, and the 19th-century former gendarmerie. Also worth seeing are the half-timbered houses on Rue du Bois Bernard and Rue du Tour des Halles, as well as the amazingly colourful ceramics at the junction of Rue Raoul Heurgault and Rue de la Place. The main attraction is the brick market hall, dating from 1836 when the textile industry and agriculture brought prosperity to the village.

When leaving why not stop by the church, where you can admire a triptych called *L'Annonciation*, a rare example of religious work by contemporary artists, signed by Philippe Gautier.

NEARBY

Saint-Aubin-de-Bonneval and Saint-Cyr-d'Estrancourt churches ㉓

61470 Avernes-Saint-Gourgon

Built with local 'grison' and cut stone, the church of Saint-Cyr-d'Estrancourt (20th century) has preserved its Romanesque portal and windows. Inside, under its open vault, it houses a rich collection of furniture and beautiful medieval statues. The nearby church of Saint-Aubin-de-Bonneval features a lovely half-timbered porch and a slate bell tower. The building is typical of the churches in Pays d'Auge.

Original speciality: apple sausage

On the occasion of the 2003 cider festival, the Le Sap butcher concocted an original speciality: apple sausage, delicately flavoured with Calvados. To learn more about these local products, a visit to the Pomme au Calvados ecomuseum is a must. Spread over 3 hectares, the museum offers insights into apple-related activities. After the visit, a gastronomic stop is recommended at the adjoining restaurant, in a delightful setting that embodies the essence of Normandy with its half-timbered houses and terracotta tiles.

Boucherie du Sap, 61470 Le Sap (commune of Sap-en-Auge)
Écomusée de la Pomme au Calvados, Rue du Grand Jardin, 61470 Le Sap
02 33 35 25 89

MARIE HAREL'S STELE

When Camembert cheese cured an American of digestive problems ...

Intersection of D246, at foot of village
61120 Camembert

One day in the Roaring Twenties an American doctor named Joseph Knirim arrived at the town of Camembert. Much to the villagers' surprise he praised the virtues of their cheese, claiming that it had cured him of a serious stomach complaint. He then launched a fundraising campaign to finance a monument in honour of this creamy delight. In 1926, a stele was erected at the road junction at the end of the village to pay tribute to Marie Harel, the woman credited with creating the famous cheese. The monument was unveiled on 20 April 1927.

Fête de la Bourgelée

Bourgelée festival, originally a pagan celebration, was Christianised by the Church. At the end of the June Mass celebrated in Église de Saint-Cyr in the town of Avernes-Saint-Gourgon, worshippers form a procession towards a field where a stack of faggots, the Bourgelée, has been piled. Once they reach their destination, they set it on fire. As it ignites, the festival king and the priest fire a shot to chase away thunder and lightning. When the flames are extinguished, each believer leaves with a piece of the embers to protect themselves from the vagaries of the elements.

Biggest eaters of Livarot cheese

Livarot cheese, named after the village where it originated a few kilometres from Camembert, is also known as the 'colonel'. Every year the village celebrates its cheese during the first weekend of August. Besides such activities as imitating pig squeals, a competition showcases the biggest eaters of Livarot cheese.

NEARBY

Pour Calvados on the grave of Mère Dornois!

Camembert cemetery
61120 Camembert

The vault of Mère Dornois, who passed away in 1915, is Camembert cemetery's absolute must-see. On her death her husband, the town mayor, poured his finest Calvados brandy into her coffin. A peculiar way to pay tribute to his wife! To perpetuate her memory, he requested that every year Calvados or another local speciality should be poured on her grave.

PRIEURÉ SAINT-MICHEL GARDENS

Former property of Edgar Chahine's family

61120 Croutes
02 33 39 15 15
Visits to priory and gardens available May–Sept, Wed–Sun 2pm–6pm

Among the meadows and valleys of Pays d'Auge, St Michael's priory, founded in the 10th century by the abbey at Jumièges, has preserved most of its buildings from the monks' time, notably the amazing tithe barn, 13th-century chapel, cellar and 15th-century press. It was owned by the family of Armenian descent of French artist Edgar Chahine (1874–1947).

The magnificent gardens, protected by hornbeam hedges, are open to visitors in summer. Stroll around the rose garden, the iris garden or the medicinal plants garden, continue along the alley of lime trees that leads to the orchard or to the wild garden bathing in waterfalls and ponds, ending at the pond of water lilies.

The luckiest can round off their walk in two guest rooms in the hostelry (14th century) or in the open suites of the old stables (18th century). Rooms are also available in two half-timbered houses dating from the

18th century, La Laiterie (for six people) and La Boulangerie (for five), next to the 13th-century chapel.

NEARBY

Troglodyte bread oven at Crouttes

The town of Crouttes owes its name to its wall recesses. One of them holds a troglodyte bread oven restored by volunteers and lit on Heritage Days.

Celtic camp of Bière

61160 Trun
Bière camp overlooks Trun plain, not far from town of Merri
Accessible all year

The Celtic camp of Bière, one of the largest in Western France (with around 50,000 cubic metres of stones), is remarkable for its proportions and state of preservation. It consists of three enclosures forming dams. The first of these, a dry-stone construction dating back to the Bronze Age, 40 metres wide and almost 7 metres high, is the most impressive. The second enclosure, made from stone and earth, is Neolithic. The third is less impressive.

LÉROT CLOCK FACE

Clock face in the shape of the Legion of Honour cross

Near church, Rue Saint-Germain
61200 Argentan

Intriguing for its shape inspired by the Legion of Honour cross, the clock overhanging Rue Saint-Germain was made by Argentan watchmaker Joseph-Richard Lérot (born 1791 in Calvados).

According to a story told around town, the watchmaker crafted it this way because he hoped to receive the prestigious Legion medal from Prince Louis-Napoléon Bonaparte on his visit to Argentan in September 1850.

Perhaps disappointed by the lack of recognition the statesman had shown him, he donated the clock face to the town in July 1854.

Greenwich meridian

The Greenwich meridian crosses France notably at Argentan, Saumur, Langon and Lourdes. A marker at the western side of town indicates the line of the meridian.

ARGENTAN
TOWN HOUSES

Rows of remarkable buildings

61200 Argentan – 02 33 67 12 48
Town plan available at municipal tourist office

Argentan is full of remarkable buildings that testify to the town's aristocratic past. To discover this rich heritage, start from Rue Saint-Germain, where at No. 11 stands the Ango de la Motte hotel. Built before 1634, this classified Historic Monument is believed to be the work of Maurice Gabriel.

Retracing your steps, take Rue du Griffon: at No. 2 is Maison Henri IV, at No. 11 is Le Brun de Breuilly hotel with its magnificent three-storey staircase tower, and at No. 24 is Bois de Belhôtel. Continue along Rue Ozenne, where you'll find Aumont de la Vente hotel where James II of England stayed in 1662.

In the same street, at No. 11, is Lepetit d'Avoines hotel (now the sub-prefecture), and at No. 13 Servain de la Chapelle hotel with its 17th-century porch. Return to Rue du Griffon, go up the street, then continue along Rue Saint-Martin towards Vigneral hotel (No. 8), Lonlay hotel (No. 24), Potier d'Yberville hotel (No. 43), and Joseph de Laleu hotel (No. 56).

Returning to Rue Saint-Germain, make a detour to Place des Vieilles Halles. There you'll find a collection of buildings, including Picot des Marais hotel (No. 1), Pitard de Cagnou hotel (Nos 3–7), Legoux hotel (Nos 9–11), Vaumelle d'Enneval hotel (No. 11), and Manoir de la Brétèche (Nos 19–21), which is now the social security office.

FRESCOES AT ARGENTAN CENTRE HOSPITALIER

Frescoes in honour of Fernand Léger

47 Rue Aristide Briand, BP 209
61200 Argentan

Celebrated artist Fernand Léger, born Argentan 1881 and died Gif-sur-Yvette 1955, lived in Argentan at his mother's house at No. 5 Rue des Jacobins. He spent part of his childhood and adolescence there until his departure for Paris in 1900. Deeply attached to his Normandy roots, he often returned to work at his Lisores farm (see p. 162) and visited his mother. All his life he advocated the use of colour to enhance the facades and decoration of buildings. As a tribute to him, a large fresco was created during the renovation of Argentan hospital, with vibrant colours identifying each department and floor. The hospital corridors are also lined with reproductions of the artist's work.

Outside, a mural commissioned from the brothers Hugues and Jean-François Sinueux also commemorates Léger's artistic legacy. It marks the entrance to the hospital at the corner of Rue des Vieilles Halles and Rue Aristide Briand with a bustling market scene including around a hundred characters, both onlookers and merchants.

NEARBY

Fresco at Argentan train station (32)

In the hall of Argentan train station, a fresco has been dedicated to Fernand Léger and filmmaker Jacques Tati, who shot one of the early scenes of *Les Vacances de Monsieur Hulot* (*Monsieur Hulot's Holiday*) there. The mural was also created by the Sinueux brothers, who had previously restored the artwork of eccentric Abbot Victor Paysant in the church at Ménil-Gondouin (see p. 122).

Jardin des Dentelles (33)

Rue Charlotte Corday, 61200 Argentan
1 April–31 May, 7am–8pm; 1 June–30 Sept, 7am–10pm; 1 Oct–31 March,
8am–6pm
The Lace Garden plantations evoke the delicate white beauty of the finest Argentan lacework. The foliage makes fine, serrated, whitish, silvery, lacy patterns. White flowers and fluffy textures further enhance the textile-inspired atmosphere. To reinforce the textile theme, flax, cotton, and mulberry trees are also growing in the park.

One tree for each child born in 2000

In the year 2000, gardeners planted a tree in Parc des Peintres (Provinces neighbourhood) to commemorate the birth of each child from Argentan. Plaques with their names were affixed to the trunks in May 2002.

BALIAS STUDIO

The artists' shelter

Château de Sérans park
61150 Écouché-les-Vallées
Daily 1 June–20 Sept and 1 Jan–30 May, 2pm–6pm
Visits to artist's studio and exhibition space by appointment

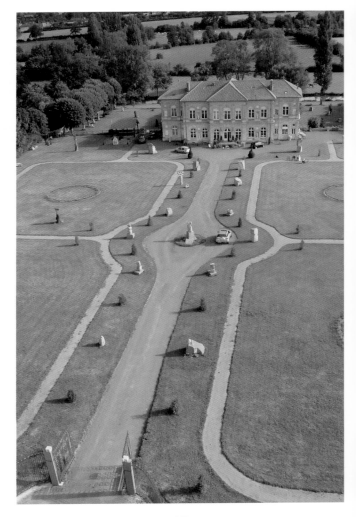

Astone's throw from the village of Écouché, a narrow country road leads to Château de Sérans, built in 1825. On arrival you have to pass through the immense gate and follow the path lined with strangely shaped sculptures accompanying you to the castle entrance.

On the porch of this magnificent residence stands the wife of Greek-born artist Balias, master of the house, who welcomes you with a smile and a hint of Swedish accent.

Inside is an exhibition gallery run by the Orne dans l'Art association, which is open to the public. But you have to book to visit the artist's studio, as well as the salon where colourful paintings with strange characters are displayed.

In the dining room an immense fresco is painted on the ceiling. The scale and richness of detail of the vibrantly coloured original work is impressive.

Outside the castle, 55 monumental sculptures of marble, granite or wood are on display in the park near a body of water. They are best appreciated early in the morning when glistening with a light layer of dew.

These works have been created by different artists from around the world at Balias' invitation.

Château de Sérans bed and breakfast
02 33 36 69 42

On the upper floor of the castle, the owners offer two charming guest rooms named Apollon and Hestia. Behind the large windows the comfort is basic, but the stopover is a chance to spend a pleasant evening with the artist. With his commanding presence and knack for witty remarks, Balias is an enjoyable companion who can engage in endless discussions on social matters.

PORCH OF CHAPELLE DE RI

An unfinished chapel

Entrance to Ri village
61210 Ri

On 6 June 1944 Abbot Leclerc, the Ri priest, had a premonition of what was about to happen in his small village. He was convinced it would find itself on the front line. To protect his parishioners he prayed for the intercession and protection of a native of the region, St John Eudes.

After fierce fighting Ri was liberated on 19 August 1944, the feast day of its protector. As a gesture of gratitude, the abbot proposed building a chapel at the entrance to the village on a plot of land spontaneously offered by a resident. The only condition set by the generous donor was that the building had to be completed within the next 25 years, otherwise the land would be reclaimed.

'Build it big enough,' advised the bishop. In 1945, a foundation stone was laid with great ceremony in the presence of notable figures of the time. But lack of funds forced the Argentan construction company entrusted with the project to close down 18 months later. The former owner, who had indeed reclaimed his property, eventually sold it to the commune. The porch still stands as a relic of a laudable intention.

Ri: homeland of St John Eudes

Inside the little church of Ri, take a moment to pray in front of the baptismal font of Église Saint-Jean-Eudes. It was here that the saint was baptised, came to know God, and received his first Communion. He returned to this church in 1637 with a mission. Indefatigable, he founded the congregation that now bears his name. He was canonised in 1925. On leaving the church you'll notice that the facade of the building opposite the Louis XVI castle is decorated with medallions representing the three Eudes brothers: Jean Eudes the religious figure, Charles Eudes d'Houay the surgeon, and François Eudes de Mézeray the historian.

PAINTED FACADE OF ÉGLISE DE MÉNIL-GONDOUIN

When the mayor walks to Rome to renovate his church

Le Bourg – 61210 Ménil-Gondouin (about 20 km from Argentan)

I n 1873, Abbot Victor Paysant (1841–1921) was ordained as parish priest of Ménil-Gondouin. He found St Vigor's church to be welcoming but

far from complete. Gradually, from 1921 onwards, the priest decided to decorate and furnish the church himself. Once the floor was completed, he gathered various religious artefacts from his pilgrimages and placed them in the nave. His place of worship, which he called a 'living and speaking church', gradually became a small 'Christian museum'.

But the priest was far from satisfied. To enliven the facade, vaulting, pavements and portal, he painted religious motifs. Unfortunately his painting skills weren't appreciated by everyone, and the bishop's office received letters of complaint from dissatisfied parishioners. Despite admonishments and warnings, the priest persevered and continued this work until his death. After 1921 Paysant's successor finally complied with the recommendations of his superiors – the statues were buried and the paintings whitewashed over.

Several years later some parishioners discovered postcards from that time. In consultation with the village elders, they decided to restore the work of the rebellious priest. In order to raise money, various activities were organised in the village, such as concerts, postcard and CD sales ... Even the local mayor joined in and set off on foot to Rome in early 2004 to collect funds.

Once the money was raised, the restoration work began with the refurbishment of the facade, which was completed in September 2004.

By 2006 the interior of the building and the stone slabs of the floor, which depict the history of humanity, had regained their former splendour.

St Vigor's was inaugurated with great pomp on 7 October 2006, by the Bishop of Sées. The church was once again open to the public, thanks to the efforts of the commune, the Amis du Houlme, and the association Les Amis de l'église parlante et vivante de Ménil-Gondouin (Friends of the speaking and living church of Ménil-Gondouin).

To round off your visit, try the publication reissued by Amis du Houlme: *L'Abbé Victor Paysant. recherches sur sa vie et son œuvre* (Abbot Victor Paysant: research on his life and work).

CRAYFISH HARVESTING

Colette's corner

Auberge d'Andaines
Route de Bagnoles
61600 La Ferté-Macé
02 33 37 20 28

Foodies have been flocking to Colette Olszowy's inn, between Bagnoles-de-l'Orne and La Ferté-Macé, since 1967. They come to savour her traditional cuisine, such as her succulent chicken fondants with porcini mushrooms and her pike fillets with vegetables. But many of them are unaware that Colette also harvests American crayfish, now plentiful in the Orne region.

In the heart of Andaines forest, Colette hunts for these crustaceans in the Villiers gorges, where she has her little corner of paradise. A little bridge overlooks a meandering river with a sandy bottom. Her fishing permit gives the restaurateur the right to set up several traps with mackerel as bait.

Back at her table, Colette gladly offers you a taste of her glass bowl of crayfish with citrus, salads and vegetables, or her sautéed crayfish and snails with a hint of tarragon. But she only reveals her secret to those who take time out to fish with her and continue the experience in the kitchen. In partnership with the departmental tourism committee, she offers packages that include a culinary discovery and a fishing session.

We must save the white-clawed crayfish!

The white-clawed crayfish (Austropotamobius pallipes) was once widespread in France.

Its numbers have however been steadily declining in recent years, especially in Orne department. The species faces numerous predators (beetles, fish, frogs, herons, mammals …), particularly targeting the youngest.

White-clawed crayfish also suffer from intense competition with their American counterparts, which are much more pollution-tolerant. These American crayfish were introduced without the knowledge that they carried a parasitic fungus (Aphanomyces astaci), responsible for crayfish plague (aphanomycosis).

Repeated surveys are crucial to safeguard this species of significant heritage value.

BELLE ÉPOQUE DISTRICT

The beautiful mansions of Bagnoles

61140 Bagnoles-de-l'Orne
Sightseeing along Christophle, Chalvet and Le-Meunier-de-la-Raillère
boulevards
Brochure available at tourist office

© André Cardeur

Albert Christophle purchased a 43-hectare plot of land not far from the thermal baths in 1886. Brilliant entrepreneur that he was, he decided to create a brand new district by building squares, grand avenues and pedestrian walkways.

Along the boulevards and behind elegant gates, he erected beautiful dwellings using wood, earth and stone. Built with local materials, these houses are also decorated with exquisite ceramics and fine features such as bow windows, turrets, canopies and roof ridges.

Along Boulevard Paul Chalvet you'll find Le Christol, a former boarding house from the 20th century; Les Hortensias, built in 1898 by entrepreneur Léon Bénard; and Le Nid Bel, two art nouveau houses.

Turning right onto Rue Auguste Bruneau towards Boulevard Albert Christophle, you'll find Le Castel, a local showhouse from 1903; Le Chalet Suédois, the former Swedish pavilion at the 1889 Universal Exhibition; and Villa Printania (1936), the most remarkable mansion on the boulevard.

LEGEND OF TOUR DE BONVOULOIR

A rather phallic structure

61140 Juvigny-Val-d'Andaine
02 33 38 40 06
3 km from Juvigny-Val-d'Andaine and 9 km west of Bagnoles-de-l'Orne: direction Chapelle Sainte-Geneviève
Free and open to visitors all year round

© Pierre Yves Beaudouin

Bonvouloir tower, near Juvigny-Val-d'Andaine in the south of the forest, is part of the remains of the castle built in 1485 by Guyon Essirard, steward to the Duke of Alençon.

Rising to a height of 26.5 metres, overlooking a smaller tower, Bonvouloir is said to have been an observation post or landmark for soldiers lost in the surrounding area.

This tower makes you think of a lighthouse. A stone staircase leads to the top, offering a remarkable panorama of the Andaine forest. But first you have to push open a heavy door with iron bands dating back 500 years.

Since the tower was first built it has been roofed with a cylindrical-conical structure, its four lookout points facing the four cardinal directions.

The Tours de Bonvouloir have been listed as Historic Monuments since 4 July 1995. A dovecote, a well, and a chapel where you can enjoy a glass of cider or perry complement this unique ensemble. The estate has belonged to the Achard de Bonvouloir family since the 16th century.

The somewhat phallic shape of the high tower has inspired a local legend. It tells the story of Lord Essirard, who despaired of not having an heir. His lady encouraged him to bathe in the waters of Tessé spring, known for restoring the life force to Lord Hugues de Tessé and his horse Rapide. Yielding to his wife's desire, after some time he finally became a father.

To commemorate his virility, Guyon Essirard had this additional tower built, so evocative in form ... The story even goes that he later had as many as 10 children.

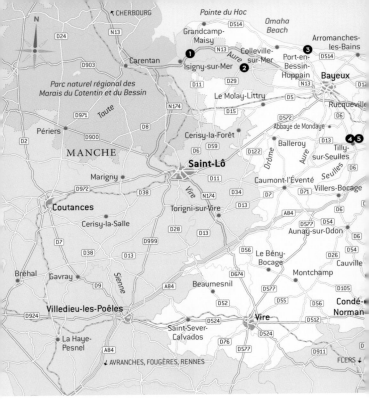

Calvados

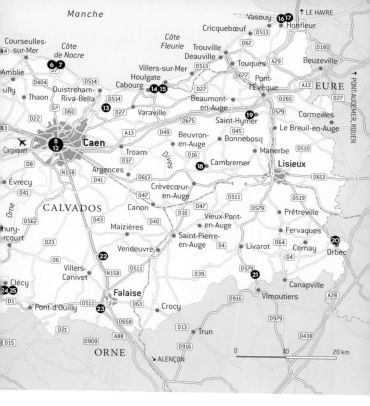

A unique garage

A few kilometres from Isigny-sur-Mer
14230 Osmanville
02 31 51 07 61
All year 2pm–7pm

There's no end to the surprises that Luc Le Gleuher springs on the folk around Osmanville. Just a stone's throw from a roundabout on Route National 13, in a small village on the borders of Calvados, near Isigny-sur-Mer, this lively Breton has settled down with his collection of vintage cars and their trappings.

Nostalgic for a particular automotive era, he gathers in his weird garage a range of objects that evoke the spirit of the 1950s, 60s and 70s. As visitors wander around, they'll come across old enamel signs bearing the names of filling stations long lost from the hall of fame. Nearby they can even play at fuel station attendant, having fun with an old pump found at the side of a country road. In the backyard, they'll step over oil cans and all sorts of old machinery, and come face to face with a vintage yellow Peugeot 404, as old as the owner's daughter. Before heading upstairs, they'll take a moment to admire the 1974 Japauto, winner of the motorcycle world championship. Then, in the gallery, they can get close to some bikes lovingly cared for by their previous owners.

Almost revelling in the smell of grease and used oil, ex-biker Le Gleuher revisits his childhood and invites his guests to do the same. Far from being a whimsical dreamer, this guy in his sixties has obtained permission to turn his collection into a proper museum: Station 70 has become the RN13 museum. While waiting for other projects to materialise, such as 'En'ville', which aims to display his collection in shop windows, Le Gleuher entrusts young apprentices with the job of restoring fine machinery at a training centre in Caen. Sometimes he even organises charitable events where people gather in work overalls sporting Ferrari caps.

TRÉVIÈRES
WAR MEMORIAL

A spectacular sculpture

14710 Trévières

arved in 1921 by former mayor Edmond Le Tual de Laheudrie, the war memorial statue in the commune of Trévières, just a few minutes away from the famous Omaha Beach, is rather spectacular. It depicts not only a woman – rare for a war memorial – but a woman disfigured by what is thought to be a cannonball.

The sculpture, wearing an Adrian helmet (see p. 70), bears the distinction of having been damaged in combat during the D-Day landings on 6 June 1944. Part of her face was blown away by a naval shell fired from nearby Omaha Beach.

In remembrance of the 1944 battles, the commune chose not to repair the statue, making the symbol of the suffering of soldiers, both men and women, even more poignant.

Fifty years later, on the 1994 anniversary of the D-Day landings, American veterans wanted to buy the statue. But the local community opposed this and it was eventually copied with the support of Calvados conseil général and Guy Wildenstein, a generous Franco-American patron. The new sculpture, named *The Lady of Trévières*, was unveiled with great pomp on 23 October 2002 by President George W. Bush. It stands at the entrance to the National D-Day Memorial in Bedford, Virginia, USA.

'DROUES' OF PORT-EN-BESSIN

Freshwater on the beach

East sea wall of Port-en-Bessin
14520 Port-en-Bessin-Huppain

The Aure river follows its course underground between Bayeux and the sea, because at Fosse Soucy, near Maisons, the water meets a natural obstacle 50 metres high, preventing it from flowing into the sea. It then infiltrates into an underground landscape carved out within layers of limestone that span over 5 km of galleries. The water finally reappears under pressure at the foot of the cliffs of Port-en-Bessin, in the form of artesian springs known as 'droues' – a freshwater source very useful to the local washerwomen.

The resurgence of the Aure at the coast can still be seen near the east sea wall of Port-en-Bessin. Here housewives would wash their laundry, much to the astonishment of strangers. When the tide went out, the washerwomen would gather at their individual exposed stones. They would kneel down and use their beater to dig a hole in the sand, which

filled with fresh water, before carrying out their unchanging rituals. The droues are particularly spectacular at low tide.

CHAPELLE
DU TRÈS-SAINT-ROSAIRE AT TILLY

A lost chapel where the Virgin Mary appeared

14250 Tilly-sur-Seulles
Sunrise to sunset
Cross the village on RD 13, heading towards Caen. After church take small
path to the right, following signboard

The Virgin Mary is said to have made a brief apparition in March 1896 on the banks of the Seulles river. She appeared to two women from the village of Tilly, Marie Martel and Louise Polinière, in front of an elm tree.

The newspapers of the time reported this event in their columns, causing a real fervour in the little village. Some came to pray to the Virgin, while others took away a leaf, branch, or piece of bark. Their adoration soon disfigured the tree.

The luckiest ones also saw the face of Our Lady. According to a local paper, the Virgin made around 20 apparitions in the field, including to students from the local private school.

A small chapel, surrounded by a white fence, now stands as testimony to this religious past. Access is via a paved alleyway. Inside the building, ex-votos are hung on the walls. Right in the middle is a small candle illuminating the statue of the Virgin, to which many worshippers still pay homage. Nearby, on the windowsill, they have placed prayers and other little messages in a school notebook.

The chapel, dating from the 1950s, was constructed on the site of a previous place of worship built in 1897 and destroyed in 1944. Even today, many people come to pay tribute to the Queen of Très-Saint-Rosaire.

NEARBY
Statue of Joan of Arc struck in the heart ⑤

Musée de la Bataille de Tilly, Chapelle Nôtre-Dame-du-Val
14250 Tilly-sur-Seulles
02 31 80 92 10
1 May–30 Sept, every weekend and public holiday 10am–midday and 2pm–6pm

A 12th-century chapel in Tilly village houses a small museum that retraces the fierce battles that took place in June and July 1944 in Tilly-sur-Seulles and the surrounding communes of Choauin, Audrieu, Hottot, Fontenay-le-Pesnel, Verrières and Villers-Bocage. Outside you can see memorials dedicated to the victims and a statue of Joan of Arc, struck in the heart by a shell fragment. The museum, now run by volunteers, aims to renew its collections.

PHARMACIE LESAGE

Art nouveau in Calvados

78 Rue du General de Gaulle – 14440 Douvres-la-Délivrande

Lesage pharmacy, listed in the Historic Monuments supplementary inventory since 7 April 1975, was built in 1901 for a certain Georges Lesage following plans drawn up by Caen-based architect François Rouvray, former pupil of the renowned art nouveau architect Hector Guimard. The wrought-iron works are by Adolphe Marie from Creully, locksmith and mechanic by trade.

Although the ensemble is strongly inspired by art nouveau, the pharmacy building, spread over three floors, is a composite of several influences. The dormer windows are Louis XIII style, the window console Louis XIV, and the stair tower on the rear facade is of medieval

inspiration. The only regrettable feature is the current windows, which have replaced the original stained glass that was of great beauty, according to the locals.

On entering the pharmacy don't miss the wooden fireplace, the counter, and the tilework with floral patterns, as well as the upper gallery made from wrought iron.

Also note the medallion on the facade, which bears inscriptions that translate as follows: 'Pharmacy Drugstore; chemicals for photography, industry and the arts; homeopathic medicines; pathological products; specialised laboratory for chemical, medical and industrial analysis; mineral waters; specialities.' It goes without saying that the pharmacist of that time was a multi-tasker!

NEARBY
Musée des manteaux de la Vierge ⑦
Basilique Notre-Dame de la Délivrande
During summer, every Tues 10am–midday and 3pm–6pm
Admission free
Visits on request at secretariat: 02 31 37 12 70

In the past, statues of the Virgin Mary were often graced with ceremonial cloaks. Notre-Dame de la Délivrande was no exception and Our Lady was dressed in various cloaks throughout the year. The remarkable Museum of the Virgin's Cloaks in Douvres-la-Délivrande houses around 15 of these pieces, generously donated by pilgrims. Notable exhibits include the cloak from the Nina Ricci workshop (1960) and the golden garment from the coronation (1872). There are also copes, chasubles and other religious artefacts worth seeing.

STAINED-GLASS WINDOWS OF ÉGLISE SAINT-JULIEN

4,500 colourful windows

1 Rue Malfilâtre – 14200 Caen
02 31 85 44 53
Every Sunday after Mass – Guided tours on reservation

St Julian's church, listed as a Historic Monument since June 2007, is a modern construction with over 1,250 square metres of reinforced concrete, 9 tonnes of steel and 4,500 stained-glass windows.

Built in 1953 by Grand Prix de Rome winner Henry Bernard, the French architect and urban planner known for rebuilding the University of Caen, the church is remarkably designed in a *mandorla* (almond) shape without a bell tower. Nestled among the houses, St Julian's needs to be seen from the inside. On entering visitors are captivated by the play of light diffused through thousands of stained-glass windows that illuminate the building. These windows were conceived by Jean Edelmann, a Parisian master glassmaker, who used 50 different shades to create his designs.

3:5 SCALE MODEL OF ANCIENT ROME

⑨

A life's work

Université de Caen Basse-Normandie
Maison de la Recherche en Sciences Humaines
Esplanade de la Paix – Campus 1
14032 Caen
Sept–July, Mon–Fri 9am–6pm
Guided tours available

In 1942 Paul Bigot passed away in Paris, leaving behind his monumental life's work: a 70-square-metre plaster 3:5 scale model representing Rome in the 4th century CE, at the time of Emperor Constantine. The model, donated to the University of Caen, is now displayed at the university's Humanities research department. Both this work and the Institut d'Art et d'Archéologie that he set up are classified as Historic Monuments.

Raymond Bigot (1872–1953), a wildlife painter and sculptor who carried off the Grand Prize at the 1925 Exposition des Arts Décoratifs, is Paul's brother.

ALCHEMICAL DECORATIONS AT HÔTEL D'ESCOVILLE

A truly philosophical residence

Hôtel d'Escoville –12 Place Saint-Pierre
14000 Caen

Hôtel d'Escoville, reconstructed after the Second World War, was originally built between 1530 and 1535 in Place Saint-Pierre at Caen. The style followed the Italianate tastes of the Renaissance and its owner, Nicolas le Valois d'Escoville (1475–1541), one of the wealthiest

merchants in town. Wealthy through a monopoly on the grain trade with Spain, d'Escoville was also a renowned alchemist who filled his home with allegories of the hermetic Great Work.

Operational alchemy (see p. 248) always requires the presence of a duality, such as Sun and Moon, subtle and dense, spirit and heart, etc. In fact, man and woman represent the perfect androgyne (the end product of the Great Work known as the Rebis), which ultimately symbolises the humanisation of the philosopher's stone. The same applies to the statues on the northern facade. On the right, King David holds the severed head of the Philistine Goliath. On the left, Judith, the widow of Esau, displays the head of Holofernes, the Assyrian general whom she seduced and beheaded. In alchemical symbolism, the severed head signifies the separation of subtle (or sacred) elements from gross (or profane) elements. In the Western tradition, biblical characters from the Old Testament are often used to reinforce the sense of primordial or ancestral state.

The five natural elements (ether, air, fire, water, earth) are also distributed on five parts of the northern facade in a significant way. Above the statue of David, two male angels support a shield bearing a coat of arms, referring to Escoville and the solar (or masculine) aspect of the Rebis. Above the statue of Judith, the scene is repeated with two female angels supporting the same coat of arms, signifying the lunar, volatile, or feminine aspect of the Rebis. Together, they represent the perfect androgyne, the philosophical adept (the alchemist), the living philosopher's stone.

Above one of the side windows stands an allegorical sculpture of a bull's head. Grids are hanging from its ears, while a staff emerges from its mouth and passes over a knife and a spit. The bull is the quintessential primal animal, representing the vital energy of nature and, in this illustration, the universal creative force known as El (God) by the ancient Hebrews. They depicted it as a complete bovine or simply as a bull's head, with bronze statuettes fixed to the end of a staff by Hebrew patriarchs from the time of Moses. Sacrificing the bull (suggested by the knife and spit) and consuming it (represented by the grids for roasting)

for alchemists meant the domination of natural forces by subjecting them to the will of the hermetic philosopher. Through successive chemical operations, by transforming their gross souls into subtle (elevated) souls, alchemists achieved the rarest state of natural elements and synthesised them into a single element called the philosopher's stone, similar to the way base 'lead' is converted into 'gold'. So the death of the bull at the hands of the alchemist equates to the 'immolation' of God (represented by wheat and grapes, eaten and drunk during the Eucharistic celebration) by the hands of man seeking to attain ultimate power and presence. The quest for the power and presence of God, with all that it entails, is depicted on the hotel's entablature. There sits the statue of a man hammering on raw material, working on visible matter to obtain the subtlety of invisible matter. He personifies the *labora* (labour) phase of alchemy, accompanied by the *ora* (meditate) phase, ensuring that the alchemical process is just and perfect. The word 'laboratory' (from the Latin words *labor* and *oratorium*) originated from the alchemists' motto *ora* et *labora* (meditate and labour).

This idea is also reflected in two small human figures carved on the entrance porch: the one on the right represents *ora*, the one on the left *labora*. Next to them is a frieze illustrating a scene from the Apocalypse, with the Scarlet Beast and the Triumphant Virgin, dominated by men and angels, and more angels in the background announcing the Celestial Jerusalem.

In alchemical symbolism, the apocalyptic beast is associated with the basilisk, a mythical creature with a bird's head and a dragon's body, which serves as precursor to the spiritual and chemical phases at the

beginning of the Great Work. The two phases together are called conjunction, and their initial stage is referred to as the Childhood of the Philosophers. Hence the panel showing a young man holding a submissive dragon by a chain. This can only be found at the entrance as it represents the early stages of the alchemical journey, as if to signpost the other stages shown inside. According to the Book of Revelation, the Scarlet Beast, representing raw matter, is associated with the number 666, which when added (6 + 6

+ 6) gives 18 and then 9 (1 + 8). This signifies the elevation of man, manifested through matter (666), to a spiritual state (999). In other words, primitive man is on the way to becoming Christian man through the transformation and transcendence of his inferior and gross (human) nature into a superior (subtle) one.

The Triumphant Virgin, with the moon at her feet, represents the soul of the world and the universe, the quintessence of matter, which alchemists recognised as the philosopher's stone. This is why Mary has always been regarded as the patroness and mother of philosophers, the deified representation of alchemy (*Allah-Chêmia* – divine chemistry in Coptic).

At the top of the entablature, next to an empty niche, two crowned serpents symbolise the fundamental masculine and feminine energies that oppose and complement each other in the Great Work, once again highlighting the presence of the hermetic duality. The celestial green serpent represents cosmic electricity known as Fohat in Hinduism, while the terrestrial red serpent signifies planetary electromagnetism referred to as Kundalini. The crowned serpents next to the niche represent the three highest elements of alchemy: sulfur, mercury and salt, which correspond to the spirit, the soul and the body of man. Traditionally, sulfur is positioned in the centre, mercury on the right, and salt on the left.

SALONS AT CALVADOS PREFECTURE

Neoclassical inspiration

Préfecture du Calvados – Rue Saint-Laurent
14000 Caen
Visits during Heritage Days only

Calvados prefecture is a remarkable building that has undergone successive reconstructions spanning more than 50 years. It stands out as one of the few French prefectures built at the very moment when prefectural authorities were established in France. A testament to neoclassical public architecture in Normandy, in a way it foreshadows the triumph of eclecticism.

In 1804, prefect Charles de Caffarelli chose the 18th-century residence of Count Gosselin de Manneville, a former mayor of Caen. The three buildings in a horseshoe shape were quickly deemed too small, prompting Napoleon I to allocate a sum of 150,000 francs for expansion works.

Architect Jean-Baptiste Harou-Romain was entrusted with the project, and the plans were finally approved in March 1812, with construction starting immediately. The wing facing the garden was completed in 1822, and the right wing in 1849. At that time the people of Caen weren't very enthusiastic about the monument. 'The prefecture building, which cost the department enormous sums, is a perfect example of modern ugliness.' This opinion expressed by Guillaume Trébutien, a friend of novelist and literary critic Jules Barbey d'Aurevilly, discredited the building for many years. Nowadays local residents have the opportunity to rediscover this architecture during Heritage Days. The most interesting elements are naturally the park, the ornamental garden, the imposing colonnade,

and the six Second Empire-style salons. Among these reception areas, the Salon des Abeilles (Salon of Bees) and the Salon Doré (Golden Salon) are the most remarkable. Their rich ornamentation evokes imperial residences.

The grand reception hall, bristling with columns, is said by specialists to be inspired by the majestic ballroom of the Château de Compiègne (Oise, northern France). On the other hand, the entrance hall with its six Doric columns reflects the Hellenistic period of classical antiquity.

RECEPTION HALL AT MAIRIE DE CAEN

⑫

Former high-school refectory

Abbaye aux Hommes – Esplanade Jean-Marie Nouvel
14000 Caen
Open during Heritage Days

The students who ate in the high-school refectory from 1804 to 1961 probably didn't pay much attention to the carved oak woodwork or the seven paintings by Lépicié, Bonnet-Dauval, Restout and the 18th-century French School. The paintings, mounted in blind apertures around the walls, are of a certain quality, especially the large canvas by Nicolas-Bernard Lépicié which shows William the Conqueror in Britain dressed as a Roman emperor.

This room, 30 metres long by 9 metres wide, was the most spacious in the Abbaye aux Hommes and already used as a refectory.

Throughout the 18th century the convent buildings were restored by the Benedictine monks of the Congrégation de Saint Maur. They were closed down at the Revolution. From 1796 they housed Calvados central school, replaced in 1804 by the imperial school of Caen, then at the Restoration by a royal college. Imperial again under the Second Empire, this became a republican establishment, taking the name of French poet François de Malherbe in 1892.

During the Second World War the buildings were converted into a hospital to save the lives of thousands of Caennais. Wartime command meetings, with maps of military operations laid out on Norman tables, were also held there. The municipal services have taken over since 1965 (the high school moved in 1961) and the rehabilitated refectory is now the city hall reception area.

MUSÉE DES ÉPIS

(13)

The heights of artisanship

Poterie du Mesnil de Bavent
14860 Ranville
02 31 84 82 41
Route départmentale 513

Mesnil de Bavent pottery, in the small town of Ranville between Caen and Le Havre, is best known for its épis de faîtage (roofing decorations). Established in 1842, this is the last remaining pottery in a region where there used to be 32. 'We are the heirs of generations of potters whose professional conscience and manual skill honour our business,' explains Dominique Kay-Mouat, the pottery manager. As advocates of artisan crafts, the potters produce roofing accessories, including ridge finials, crested ridge tiles, and interior or exterior architectural elements. They also create life-sized ceramic animals such as cats, dogs, hens and roosters.

The Bavent pottery is now sought out by the Historic Monuments organisation to restore the finials (roof crowns made from enamelled or unglazed terracotta) on traditional Norman residences. In 2007 its rare expertise was recognised by the label Entreprise du Patrimoine Vivant (Living Heritage Company).

Visits to the workshops and a small museum showcasing both antique and contemporary pieces are organised throughout the year. Occasional exhibitions are held on the premises, much to the delight of enthusiasts.

LEPER HOLE

Unwanted worshippers

Église de Dives-sur-Mer, 14160 Dives-sur-Mer
Occasional guided tours organised
Enquire at tourist office: 02 31 91 24 66

In principle every leper colony had its chapel, but for those without one a space known as the 'leper hole' was often made in the wall of the nearest church. This practice, of course intended to prevent any contamination, allowed leprosy victims to follow the service from outside. At the back right of the Dives church, such an opening still exists. This small window is wide on the outside and narrows on the inside, forming a slit through which only two or three of the afflicted could listen to the sermons. As an additional curiosity, the hole was designed in such a way that it directed their gaze towards the miraculous Christ at the heart of the church. The hole, sealed in 1696 when the neighbouring leper colony closed down, was rediscovered in 1974 by the parish priest.

Other leper holes

In the churches at Urrugne, La Bastide-Clairence and Ascain there were similar doors and holy water stoups reserved for lepers (see *Pays basque insolite et secret*, also published by Jonglez). In Aizier, relics of the former leper colony can still be seen at Chapelle Saint-Thomas (see p. 192).

Fans of French author Marcel Proust will recognise this place as the church at Balbec, the fictional town in his novel *À la recherche du temps perdu* (*In Search of Lost Time*).

MAISON BLEUE

An extraordinary garden

Rue des Frères Bisson, 14160 Dives-sur-Mer
Open certain dates for guided tours: check with tourist office:
02 31 91 24 66

The Blue House, built between 1957 and 1984 by Euclides da Costa Ferreira, is a heterogeneous ensemble of house, garden, chapels and miniature mills. Its structures, walls, floors and furniture are completely covered with ceramics, or even salvaged glass.

Property of the commune of Dives since 1989 and included in the additional inventory of Historic Monuments in 1991, the Blue House has recently been restored. Workers from the local region have taken every precaution in the world to save these miniature buildings.

The first of them, a mausoleum to the glory of Laika, was inspired by the sacrifice of the first living being sent into orbit around the Earth. The dog died of stress seven hours after her launch into space. The first Soviet accounts implied that she had been poisoned by spoiled food. Nearby is Notre-Dame de Lourdes, a tiny chapel with a statue of Our Lady of Lourdes on top of the porch and a cave strewn with large pebbles alongside. Notre-Dame de Fatima, the original version of which is venerated in Costa Ferreira's native Portugal, was built in 1962. The entrance is up three small steps, one with the mosaic inscription 'Fatima'. All this is dominated by a bell tower and pyramid. The Sacré-Coeur (Sacred Heart) largest of the small buildings, dating from 1965, is reinforced by bell-shaped buttresses. Finally, Sainte-Rita de Cascia (1967), the fourth chapel on the site, is tinted blue and decorated with an extraordinary bestiary.

PETIT MUSÉE
D'ALPHONSE ALLAIS

Love of humour

10 Rue des Petites Boucheries
14660 Honfleur
Tours on reservation: 06 74 07 72 29

The story of this amazing museum begins a few streets away, on the upper floor of the now-closed Passocéan pharmacy near Honfleur port. The famous journalist, poet and humorist Alphonse Allais came into the world there.

His father was the owner, and there Alphonse engaged in his early pranks, staining his neighbours' laundry and amusing his friends with pharmaceuticals from the shop. One day he even made 'scammony biscuits', a powerful and almost instantaneous purgative handed out to his classmates.

In 1935, a curious character named Paul Démarais bought Alphonse's father's pharmacy. This apothecary, well known in Honfleur, was among other things candidate for the presidency of the Republic in 1939, inventor of an unusual method for learning English, and director of the *Journal des écrasés de la nation* (Journal of the nation's oppressed). He was seen as a kind man who didn't hesitate to help the most deprived with charitable works. He also devised a remedy for pimples and skin rashes and a lotion to stop hair turning grey.

Among all these roles he was, 'in all seriousness', commander of the Grand Humanitarian Prize of Belgium, honorary member of Venice Academy, commander of the World Order of Human Merit, and held the cross of honour as officer of the Humanitarian Works of Toulouse. His overflowing imagination and eccentric character fed a megalomania that only the Bon Sauveur psychiatric hospital in Caen was able to treat. For many years, the pharmacy perpetuated this humorous tradition by displaying Alphonse Allais' inventions in cabinets on the second floor, all of which are now relocated to the new museum at 10 Rue des Petites Boucheries.

The eclectic collection includes Voltaire's skull at the age of 17; an authentic piece from the fake Cross of Jesus Christ; a cup with the handle on the left, specially made for a left-handed Ming emperor; and blue, white and red starch for keeping flags unfurled on windless days. The curator-guide, Jean-Yves Loriot, offers tours on reservation around this unique collection, whose new premises were chosen as 'a place where Alphonse didn't go'.

LA FORGE HOME WORKSHOP

'My house is a work of art in itself'

45 Rue de la Foulerie
14600 Honfleur
06 44 03 70 33
laforge-honfleur.com
Guided tours by Florence Marie, every Fri, Sat and Sun 3pm–5pm, and on reservation other days

A visit to Florence Marie's home workshop in the heart of Honfleur, just a stone's throw from the old harbour, is an initiatory journey into the imagination of an always-inspired artist.

The house is named La Forge in tribute to the previous owner, a carpenter who forged his own tools. The artist has lived and worked there since 1995, dedicating her time to an ever-evolving work of art.

The surrounding garden contributes greatly to the atmosphere. Florence Marie discovered an underground passage in the depths of the garden, from which a lively spring feeds two basins and a washhouse. At the end of the passage, carried along by the haunting trickle of a fountain, you'll glimpse an eternal woman with green eyes, both welcoming and fearful.

This secret garden reveals itself step by step, inviting visitors into astonishing worlds filled with the artist's imagination, interior and exterior constantly echo each other. For example, the large green fresco in the garden extends into the library, on the coffered ceiling made from dried fish boxes. In the garden, trees, bushes and flowers communicate with sculptures, mosaics and frescoes.

This phantasmagorical world was born from a simple fresco originally designed to hide an unsightly wall in the garden.

Florence Marie's aesthetic approach revolves around monumental sculptures exploring animal forms (giraffe, elephant, dinosaurs, whale) and symbolic constructions.

Her creations, preferably in recycled materials, continue the tradition of classic tales intertwined with her personal mythology, while following in the tracks of artists such as Facteur (Postman) Cheval, Niki de Saint Phalle, Robert Tatin and Picassiette (Raymond Isidore, mosaic creator).

Within this garden maintained by volunteers, the apparent botanical anarchy conceals a scientific inventory of flora and a great respect for the environment.

This place, already classified as *Art singulier* (Unique art), hopes to soon obtain the label *Jardin remarquable* (Remarkable garden).

CAMBREMER CLOCK FACE

A clock without a mechanism

Clock face at outskirts of village, at Saint-Jean crossroads heading towards Caen
14340 Cambremer
15 km from Lisieux

The village with its wood and brick houses, as well as its tithe barn, nestles around a 12th-century Romanesque church. The commune is the capital of cider and Calvados, on sale at an old-style market every Sunday morning in July, August, Easter and Pentecost. It's also the starting point for tourist trails: the cider trail, the *douets* (streams) trail, the marshes trail and the cheese trail.

At the outskirts of the village, on the way to Caen, is an old house graced with a splendid clock face. Despite its size, the clock has never shown the right time simply because it lacks a working mechanism. This curiosity is easily explained by the history of the building. The house, at the junction of departmental roads 85 and 50, used to be a coaching inn. The clock hands were manually moved only to announce the departure and arrival of the next mail coaches.

> Cambremer inspired several passages of Marcel Proust's novel *À l'ombre des jeunes filles en fleurs* (*Within a Budding Grove*).

NEARBY
Tomb of Mère Denis

Saint-Hymer cemetery – 14130 Saint-Hymer (a few kilometres south of Pont-l'Évêque)

Mère Denis, real name Jeanne-Marie Le Calvé, was born near Pontivy in 1890 in Morbihan region. After a difficult childhood marked by poverty and hunger, she was placed in a household at the age of 11 and married at 17. She worked as a level-crossing keeper near Barneville-Carteret, Manche, before resigning to become a washerwoman at the Gerfleur laundry from 1944 to 1963. In retirement she faced financial hardship until her neighbour, Pierre Baton, a publicist, offered her the opportunity to promote a washing machine. So at the age of 79 she began a successful TV career, immortalised by advertising campaigns for the *Vedette* brand. Her laughter and catchphrases, such as 'ch'est ben vrai cha!' ('That's absolutely true, that is!') became famous in small-screen history. Mère Denis passed away in 1989 at Pont-l'Évêque and now lies at rest in Saint-Hymer cemetery, not far from a beautiful priory and a gently meandering stream.

ORBEC WATERMILL

One of the eight water-raising machines built in France

Petit Moulin d'Orbec
15 Rue Saint-Pierre, 14290 Orbec
06 09 85 61 66
lepetitmoulin-orbec.fr – lepetitmoulin.orbec@gmail.com
Guided tours by owners, available throughout the year on reservation

The Petit Moulin, documented since the 12th century, was one of 17 mills that provided Orbec's water service in 1880. The drinking water supply for the 3,000 residents was far from satisfactory, as the water from the streams that criss-crossed the town was polluted from indiscriminate dumping.

Only four public wells with wooden pumps provided access to spring water. To address this problem, the commune enlisted the services of engineer Ernest-Sylvain Bollée from Le Mans, who installed a water-raising machine at the Petit Moulin in 1883.

Two reservoirs were used to supply water to 30 public fountains, fire hydrants, and two washhouses around the town, ensuring access to good quality spring water for all.

Auguste-Sylvain Bollée, Ernest's brother and a windmill manufacturer, provided the pumps to extract water from the basin fed by the Saint-Pierre and Bibet springs.

The machine and kilometres of pipelines to supply water to the town were delivered at Orbec railway station on the Lisieux-Orbec line, opened a few years earlier.

Among the eight such machines built in France, this is the only one that can be seen in such a well-preserved state and capable of working once more.

A dynasty of inventors

The Bollée family formed a veritable dynasty of inventors in 19th-century Le Mans. Father Ernest-Sylvain Bollée and his three sons, Amédée-Ernest Bollée Sr, Ernest-Jules Bollée and Auguste-Sylvain Bollée, held over 700 patents in various fields, including the hydraulic industry, windmills, and steam- and gasoline-powered automobiles. Ernest-Sylvain was responsible for developing windmills, such as the one at Mesnil d'Acon in Eure (see p. 242).

FERME-MUSÉE FERNAND LÉGER

The painter emerges from oblivion

14140 Lisores
April–Sept
Entire access path can be viewed

I n the hollow of a valley in Lisores, the Normandy farmhouse of Fernand Léger (1881–1955) was abandoned and overgrown with brambles and nettles.

From the path leading to the house, only one large mosaic fresco by the artist could be seen on the front wall, still standing among the wild grass, climbing moss and scattered stones.

Over a number of years the workshop of one of the world's greatest artists had fallen into complete oblivion, much to the dismay of the locals. With heavy hearts, they hoped for intervention from the state, the region and the department to save this heritage.

In the absence of public assistance, the town of Lisores eventually found an art dealer, Jean du Chatenet, who bought the property in 2007 and cleared the land.

Through hard work (nearly three years as a building site), the new owner managed to bring the artwork on the gable end out of the shadows.

Named La Fermière et sa vache (The farmer and her cow), it remains intact despite a few shotgun pellets fired by hunters.

This scene covers a large surface of 20 square metres – the original gouache was given to a certain Maurice Thorez.

From 1955 to 1982 Léger used this farmhouse as his studio and living space, and built the small chapel in the 3-hectare park himself.

Peasant painter

Fernand Léger felt a strong attachment to his native region, where he made ceramics and stained glass. Born on 4 February 1881 in Argentan, he started out as apprentice to an architect in Caen before heading for Paris at the age of 19. He abandoned architecture and began associating with Chagall, Cendrars, Max Jacob and Modigliani. In the 1930s the artist, known as the 'peasant of the avant-garde', gained international fame. He went to the USA and lived there until 1945. On his return to France, Léger created numerous monumental works until his death in 1955. He is now celebrated worldwide, with a national museum dedicated to him at Biot in south-eastern France.

TOMB OF ACTRESS MARIE JOLY

A replica of Jean-Jacques Rousseau's tomb

La Brèche au Diable, 14420 Soumont-Saint-Quentin
Between Tassilly and Soumont-Saint-Quentin, 9 km north of Falaise

The Laizon is a small river that winds through hills of Armorican sandstone. It carves its way through a pleasant location called La Brèche au Diable (The Devil's Gap), 9 km from Falaise, near Soumont-Saint-Quentin and not far from Tassilly.

It's said that on this spot the Devil, in a fit of anger, split the earth with a swipe of his tail. To find this majestic natural site, starting from the church at Potigny, go up Rue du Tiais, then turn right at the departmental road. Cross the road before ascending Chemin des Roches. La Brèche au Diable is an oasis of greenery that leads to a bare wall of rock bearing a tomb where actress Marie Joly, born in Versailles on 8 April 1761, lies at rest.

As a member of the Comédie-Française she portrayed Dorine in Molière's *Tartuffe* (*The Imposter*) and Toinette in *Le Malade imaginaire* (*The Imaginary Invalid*). With fragile health, the actress died young in 1798. Her wealthy husband erected a tomb for her, which is an exact replica of the great philosopher Jean-Jacques Rousseau's tomb (see photos opposite).

A truly romantic place, it features a beautiful epitaph on the west side of her tomb: 'She is no more, this adorable woman / Favourite of games, graces and loves / Joly is no more. The inexorable Fate / Has severed the thread of her days

TOMBEAU DE JEAN JACQUES ROUSSEAU
Vue de l'Isle des Peupliers, dite l'Elisée, partie des Jardins d'Ermenonville dans laquelle J.J. Rousseau, mort à l'âge de 66 ans, a été enterré le 4 Juillet 1778

CHAPELLE SAINT-VIGOR

23

A Japanese artist in the Normandy bocage

14627 Saint-Martin-de-Mieux
5 km from Falaise, towards Condé-en-Normandie
15 June–15 Sept 2.30pm–6pm, daily except Mondays

Saint-Vigor-de-Mieux chapel, lost in the wooded countryside (bocage) 5 km south-west of Falaise, is truly ageless. Locals claim that it was built in the 15th century. The chapel, in danger of falling into ruin, owes its restoration to Japanese painter Kyoji Takubo, who undertook a colossal project with the help of local residents. This artist, who is also an architect, had the idea of covering the roof with colourful glass tiles. Created by master glassmaker Olivier Juteau, these tiles were placed among the older tiles, forming a beautiful mosaic that illuminates the chapel as soon as the sun appears. Inside, don't miss the chestnut woodwork and the walls painted with apple tree branches.

The chapel has now become a venue for exhibitions and cultural exchanges, aimed at fostering Franco-Japanese relations in the Normandy *bocage*.

MUSÉE DU CHEMIN DE FER MINIATURE

24

Models galore

Rue d'Ermington
14570 Clécy
02 31 69 07 13
March, Sun 2pm–5.30pm
Easter–May, daily 10am–midday and 2pm–6pm
June, Tues–Sun 2pm–6.30pm
1–15 Sept, Tues–Sun 10am–midday and 2pm–6pm
16–30 Sept, Tues–Sun 2pm–6pm
Oct, Sun 2pm–5.30pm

Since 1970, the Miniature Railway Museum has been offering an astonishing spectacle that leaves both young and old in awe. Over some 450 metres of track, 260 Lilliputian locomotives race through small houses and industrial sites. In this mini railway world, every detail is important: a ringing telephone booth, smoking chimneys, twirling skaters, whistling stationmasters …

Nostalgic visitors can relive memories of old trains, back when compartments displayed black and white photos of French villages. The spectacle is especially picturesque at nightfall, when the lights twinkle brightly.

MUSÉE ANDRÉ HARDY

Forgotten agricultural France

Place du Tripot
14570 Clécy
02 31 69 79 95
April–Sept, Tues–Fri 10am–12.30pm, Sat 10am–12.30pm and 2.30pm–
5.30pm; July and Aug, Mon–Sun 10am–12.30pm and 2.30pm–6.30pm

Place du Tripot in Clécy, deep in Suisse Normande (area of country that resembles the Swiss Alps), resonates like an Audiard movie soundtrack. Imagine shady cafés where young women indulge in carnal pleasures. But no, this flower-filled square is actually a small haven of peace where you'll find the André Hardy museum. To visit, request a key from the tourist office and climb the stairs two at a time. In a small room around a hundred drawings, watercolours and paintings showcase the artist's work.

The collection might not be exceptional yet it depicts a forgotten France, the world of the surrounding agricultural community.

VIRGIN OF THE YEW TREE

A strange cult

Église de Saint-Rémy-sur-Orne
14570 Saint-Rémy-sur-Orne

I n the heart of the Suisse Normande massif, a winding road leads to a monumental yew tree blocking the path of passers-by. Standing at a

height of 18 metres (13 metres tall in 1930) and with a diameter of 6.7 metres, the tree shelters a white and blue Virgin Mary statue placed on a wooden pedestal.

In the 18th century a small chapel was even built inside the hollow trunk. Until one day the congregation decided to remove it as the candle flames had almost set their tree on fire the previous evening.

Statuettes, marble ex-votos and rosaries were left in the sanctuary but gradually disappeared over the course of the 20th century. Before leaving, take a look inside the church topped with a gabled tower. The choir is decorated with murals painted in 1895 by an artist named Chiffrey.

Ancient yews of Normandy

The Normandy region is the hideaway of France's largest concentration of ancient yew trees, known to be trees planted in cemeteries (see p. 197). In Manche department they can be found near St Ursin's church, in the cemetery at Brix and near the church at La Bloutière.

In Calvados, you'll find a few more in the cemeteries of Castillon, Courson, Estry, Pierres and Saint-Pierre-la-Vieille. Additionally, in Orne there's a yew in the cemetery of La Lande-Patry, another in Lalacelle, and Eure has two millennial yews at La Haye-de-Routot (see p. 196).

NEARBY

Druid stone: temple for pagan worshippers

On the heights of Périgny
14770 Saint-Pierre-la-Vieille

Not far from Saint-Pierre-la-Vieille, in the undulating landscape of Suisse Normande, Périgny offers cascading scenery, small verdant paths, and rocks of sandstone and shale. Far from everything, this small Calvados commune has become a temple for pagan cult fans, and not without reason. Hidden among a tangle of undergrowth lies a Druid stone, the legendary refuge of a fantastic beast called the '*codrille*'. This Norman werewolf haunting the groves is said to frighten those who seek it out. The creature sometimes takes flight and disappears into the sky for a while when no longer bothered by visitors. But beware ... it's never far away. With long strides, it bounds back to haunt its rock, whistling lugubriously and 'scratching' the stone.

CALVARY OF CONDÉ-EN-NORMANDIE

Plague buboes

Square de la Cour du Roy
14110 Condé-en-Normandie

Between July 1626 and December 1627 there were approximately 400 plague victims in the town of Condé-sur-Noireau (renamed Condé-en-Normandie in 2016). To invoke the healing saints, St Sebastian and St Roch, the people of Condé-en-Normandie erected a calvary in the cemetery surrounding the church of Saint-Martin.

In 1924 the monument was moved to the crossroads (Carrefour des trois passes) during the construction of the First World War memorial. It was damaged during the 1999 storm but later restored and reinstalled in its original location, in the middle of Square de la Cour du Roy. The granite pedestal features eight buboes, symbolising the disease.

A chalet donated by Sweden, converted into a nursery

In June 1944, Condé-sur-Noireau was 95 per cent destroyed by bombing. For rebuilding, the town benefited from the generosity of Sweden, a neutral country during the global conflict of 1939–45. In 1946 it was granted 60 houses out of the 400 offered to Calvados department by a Swedish royal decree dated 15 March. These 'Swedish chalets' made from wood were designed by architect Sven Ivar Lind. They are single-storey and reflect the style of houses in the Normandy region, the only difference being their steep roofs. They were equipped with all mod cons of the time, such as fitted kitchen, central heating, shower, toilet and laundry room.

As the icing on the 'rebuilding' cake, Condé also acquired a temple and a nursery. The 'pink nursery' (its colour) was established on Boulevard du 11 Novembre. Like its counterparts in Caen and Colombelles, in the first year of operation, 1948, the nursery was run by both Swedish and French personnel. Designed by Sven Ivar Lind, the 'baby house' consisted of a long wooden building with stone foundations and basements. The rest, including prefabricated elements, furnishings and equipment (bedding, playpens, toys, etc.), was planned and supplied by the Swedes.

Until the end of 2004, the nursery housed the headquarters of the Association des Familles Rurales, which ran a daycare and leisure centre. Local associations now occupy the premises.

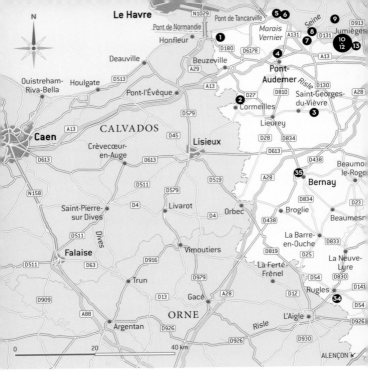

Eure

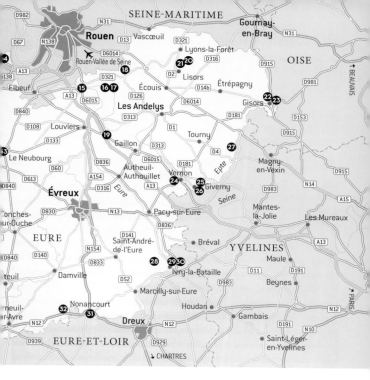

ROOMS AT FATOUVILLE-GRESTAIN LIGHTHOUSE

Sleep in a lighthouse

27210 Fatouville-Grestain
Anne and Jean-François Durand
02 32 57 66 56 / 06 89 23 56 59

The '*Bonhomme de Fatouville*', or '*Homme des bois*', is what sailors heading up the Seine estuary (which used to be extremely dangerous due to the number of shifting sandbanks) call a fir tree with a human look that indicated the route to follow.

A pilot who had spent his life guiding ships in the estuary is thought to have planted the tree, which gradually took the form of a hunchbacked old man wearing a wide-brimmed hat – what sailors call an *amer*.

When this tree was brought down by a storm the decision was made to replace it to protect navigation in the Seine. What is now Fatouville-Grestain lighthouse was built on a green islet together with a series of other lights at the edge of the cliff.

The Fatouville lighthouse, completed in 1850, was different in height and importance to other lighthouses that marked the Seine. But it suffered from a major drawback: when there was fog in the valley, which is common, it was invisible. So it was replaced in the early 20th century by electric lighting on the banks of the Seine.

The lighthouse, decommissioned in 1908, was sold in 1923 to Gaston David, the current owner's grandfather. In one of the sections he opened four guest rooms, including one for a family of four. Although the rooms are unfortunately not at the top of the lighthouse, as you might have hoped, access to the top is possible for guests – a small privilege that alone almost justifies sleeping there. Better still, they can even breakfast under the dome.

The panorama over Honfleur, the Seine estuary and Pont de Normandie road bridge is exceptional – from a height of 32 metres up 164 steps.

You can visit the lighthouse free of charge on certain Thursdays between March and October.

Fatouville is one of only two French lighthouses that welcome guests. The other is Kerbel lighthouse in Morbihan department.

SENTIER DE LA BIODIVERSITÉ

Discovering the natural treasures of Normandy's bocage

Starting from Cormeilles, pick up a leaflet describing the trail at tourist office of Cormeilles canton, at 21 Place du Général de Gaulle, and park near water tower – one of the access points to biodiversity trail is nearby
Be sure to wear sturdy walking shoes and bring rain gear
Hiking trail covers 6 km and is steep in parts
02 32 56 02 39
cormeilles.com

Cormeilles 'biodiversity trail' is one of the most pleasant and lesser-known walks you can take to discover Normandy's deeply wooded countryside known as bocage.

Along its 6 km of sunken paths, what Normans call '*cavées*', you'll come across a succession of flora and fauna characteristic of wetlands and other environments. The Douet-Tourtelle, a tributary of the Calonne river, which in turn flows into the Touques river, crosses the trail twice. In the surrounding meadows you'll find reeds and wild watercress,

green or red tree frogs, trout and sticklebacks, not to mention voles and shrews. Fearing herons, buzzards and humans, these animals hide, but if you know how to be quiet and surprise them, you might be lucky enough to spot them.

The canopies of old pollarded trees, often weathered and hollow, provide a remarkable habitat (great spotted woodpecker, little owl, white-faced redstart), while on the ground, beneath the shade of lime, ash, oak, beech and field maple trees, a unique vegetation thrives: wild garlic, Solomon's seal, herbe aux femmes battues (black bryony, known for its curative roots), etc.

The characteristic hedgerows of the bocage landscape harbour several layers of vegetation: mosses, ferns and flowering plants, shrubs (hawthorn, holly, butcher's broom, boxwood, hazel ...), and the trees mentioned.

Animals such as hedgehogs, goldfinches or cuckoos take advantage of the hedgerow to nest or feed.

Through panoramic openings along the trail you'll gain a better understanding of the still extraordinary biodiversity of the bocage. A real pleasure, away from the heat and crowds of summer.

RIDDLE OF ÉGLISE DE SAINT-GRÉGOIRE-DU-VIÈVRE FACADE

The Christian world is corrupted ...

27450 Saint-Grégoire-du-Vièvre
Check opening hours at commune of Saint-Georges-du-Vièvre tourist office:
02 32 56 34 29
saintgeorgesduvievre.org

On the south wall of Saint-Grégoire-du-Vièvre village church (first half of 16th century) are some very curious inscriptions – an alternating pattern of white stones and carved black flint (arranged in a chequerboard pattern), flint stones in the shape of crosses, figures, animals, and finally inscriptions that seem to form a graphic riddle.

The translation of this riddle made by Join Lambert in 1888, 'The Christian world is corrupt and wrong,' would according to the authors

denounce what Christianity had become after eradicating the Celtic religion (see following double-page spread).

Next are the suggestive figures of two animals fighting, probably representing the opposing and irreconcilable natures of the Celtic and Christian religions.

Christianity is represented by another human figure inciting a dog to attack a wolf, which eventually dies.

The human figure could represent the Christian clergy, the dog symbolising the loyalty of the Church's servants, and the wolf the persecuted and condemned Celtic religion.

Lastly there are graffiti of a knight on foot chasing after his fleeing horse. This message is certainly simple and more critical. The order of Christian chivalry has lost its tradition of chastity and has been corrupted by the immorality of worldly vices, together with the clergy's break with the spirit of true Christianity.

Despite the esoteric interpretations that some claim for these graffiti, they are primarily a written protest in the form of an enigma against the abuse of power and the intolerance of the dominant religion.

St Ursin: a saint for stomach ailments, derived from the ancient Celtic religion

Saint-Grégoire-du-Vièvre, in Normandy, is believed to be the meeting point between Pope St Gregory the Great (c. 540–12 March 604) and a dragon from French folklore, the vièvre (vouivre). It's not clear who charmed or converted whom because the two characters represent, respectively, the imported Christian religion and the indigenous Celtic religion. What is known is that initially the two religions coexisted with great mutual respect. Only later, with the conversion of the Roman Empire to Christianity, did bloody persecutions take place against Celtic priests and Druids and the suppression of their religion. Nevertheless its memory and tradition survived in hidden ways within Christian hagiography. The church of Saint-Grégoire-le-Grand was built in the first half of the 16th century and reconstructed the following century, but it was based on a chapel that already existed in the 10th century (in the lost forest of Vièvre). The chapel was dedicated to another patron saint, Ursin, who was known for curing stomach ailments. 'Saint Ursin' literally means 'holy bear', the emblematic animal of the Celtic world. The warrior class, which referred to the bear as *artos* (in Breton, *arzh*), attributed it with sanctity and even immortalised it in

the Great Bear and Little Bear constellations. The feminine or passive nature of the warrior caste, in contrast to the priestly authority of the Druids, led to the sacred invention of a Celtic goddess called Artis, meaning 'bear'. This goddess possessed the ability to heal the wounds of warriors injured in battle, particularly wounds to the stomach, which was considered the psycho-emotional centre of the human body associated with femininity. And so with the conversion to Christianity the holy bear became St Ursin ... But the original religion persisted, represented by the dragon (*vièvre*), and early Roman Christianity imposed the figure of St Gregory as a symbol of conversion through force, or rather as St George the dragon slayer.

The church has some other peculiarities. While in most churches the baptismal fonts stand on the left as you enter, here they are on the right. This is because an underground river running beneath the left side is thought to have affected the layout. Similarly, the patron saint of the church is typically found on the left side of the altar, but in this case St Gregory is on the right, allowing St Joseph to take the place of honour. Finally, the flint escutcheon on the exterior is probably an element of the seigneurial livery, usually painted either inside or outside churches.

ROMANESQUE TOWER OF SAINT-MARDS-DE-BLACARVILLE

A church converted into an English-style cottage

27500 Saint-Mards-de-Blacarville
Starting from Pont-Audemer, take D39 towards Saint-Samson-de-la-Roque,
which runs along right bank of Risle river – just after bridge under Normandie
autoroute, park at 'la Vallée'
Visible from outside, from road, and even from autoroute
Closed to the public

In 1835 the merger took place of the two communes of Saint-Mards-sur-Risle and Blacarville, whose two churches dated back to the Romanesque period. The church of Blacarville being larger, the church of Saint-Mards was sold.

In 1892 the nave was demolished, but the choir and tower were preserved and converted into an English-style cottage. In the process, the tower lost its roof to make way for battlements that had never existed before, aiming to evoke a defensive structure.

This is now referred to as the 'Romanesque tower'. At its base there used to be a mill, and you can still see the canal that carried water to the place where the waterwheel originally stood. While the conversion of a church into a home is nothing out of the ordinary, as also seen at Saint-Aubin-de-Quillebeuf (Chapelle Saint-Léonard) or Tancarville (the old church), this one was nevertheless very early.

St Mards is another name for St Medard (or Medardus).

St Medard

St Medard was a Frankish noble known for his great compassion towards the less fortunate. He became bishop of Noyon (northern France) in 530 and later of Tournai. Legend has it that he gave a horse to a man who had lost his own, and miraculously, when returning the horses to his father, none of them were missing.

The legend also tells that he was protected from the rain by an eagle that spread its wings above him. As a result he is invoked by farmers as the bringer of rain. The popular saying goes: 'If it rains on St Medard's day (8 June), it will rain for 40 more days (until 18 July), unless St Barnabas (11 June) takes the grass from under his feet.'

BOAT GRAFFITI AT QUILLEBEUF

'Who holds Quillebeuf holds Paris'

Église de Quillebeuf, 27680 Quillebeuf-sur-Seine
Take A131 autoroute, then D87 or D110 and ferry from Notre-Dame-de-
Gravenchon, park in lighthouse parking lot
Church key can be obtained from town hall on weekdays (9am–5pm) and from
Coccimarket grocery store on Rue du Marché at weekends
A guided tour circuit, including panels and plaques on the most interesting
houses, and free visitor leaflet (available at town hall: 02 32 57 51 25;
or Bourneville Canton tourist office: 02 32 57 32 23)

O nce capital of Roumois region in north-western Eure, the town of
Quillebeuf is now completely forgotten, located as it is away from
major routes with an unattractive industrial presence. It's not a place
you pass through; you need a reason to go there!

Who remembers that it was once a major port on the Seine and a
disputed stronghold? The town was won over to the Protestant cause
and rewarded by Henry IV, who granted it the monopoly over Seine
boat piloting and fortified it, even naming it Henricarville.

Until the development of the Seine from 1848 onwards, almost all

boats travelling up or down the river towards Rouen, Paris or beyond had to stop at Quillebeuf due to sandbars on either side of town.

Also in bad weather it wasn't uncommon for ships to be stranded in Quillebeuf for several days. This brought prosperity to the town, and architectural testimonies of that era can still be found along the main street, where a collection of houses from the 16th to the 18th centuries showcases uniquely interesting features.

Take the time to examine them in detail, as some of these houses have engraved texts on their beams. For example, the '*maison du paradis*' bears the inscription: 'A man living with justice and reason, serving God in deeds and words, good people will say that his house here on Earth is a little paradise.'

Explore the open courtyards that are accessible to visitors and discover the boat graffiti around the walls. Finally, return via the narrow street called '*Casse-cou*' (Daredevil) and the path known as '*Comte Maurice*' (Count Maurice), which overlook the main street and offer a panoramic view of the Seine.

Boat graffiti

The boat graffiti, along with engravings and paintings, provide valuable insights into the world of small fishing and commercial vessels, for which pre-18th century documentation is scarce. Thousands of boat graffiti can be found in the lower Seine valley, decorating both civil and religious buildings. These cannot be considered votive, as paper was scarce at that time. The study of their placement on walls leads to hypotheses about the time or season they were carved. It also provides clues about the tools used and the probable size of whoever engraved them. They were probably created by sailors waiting to board ship, as some of the technical details shown would have been known only to seafarers.

NEARBY

A visit to Notre-Dame de Bon-Port church, with its magnificent Romanesque bell tower, is highly recommended. The church houses several ex-votos (ship models and paintings), impressive boat graffiti in terms of size, and a recent collection of model boats that evokes the history of navigation on the Seine in the 18th and 19th centuries.

MODEL OF THE *TÉLÉMAQUE*

The hidden treasure of Norman abbeys taken away in secret during the Revolution?

27680 Quillebeuf-sur-Seine
From A131 autoroute take D87, or via D110 and ferry from Notre-Dame-de-Gravenchon, to lighthouse parking lot

In Quillebeuf church, the modern model of a ship recalls a remarkable episode in French history.

On 3 January 1790 the brig *Télémaque*, renamed Quintanadoine, broke its moorings in Quillebeuf and ran aground in the port during the night. Within hours it was rolled over by the tidal bore and sucked into the shifting sands. The authorities were suspicious of the ship. It had left Rouen for Brest on 1 January, after loading barrels declared to be filled with nails and tallow, but suspected of containing coins and jewels instead.

The authorities in Quillebeuf were then ordered to intercept it. Meanwhile, the captain of the *Télémaque* was instructed not to make any stops on the Seine. He also carried an envelope indicating his final destination, which he could only open once at sea. There were suspicions that, under the guise of transporting wood, the *Télémaque* was carrying the belongings of emigrating nobles, and perhaps even those of Louis XVI, as well as the treasure of Norman abbeys.

A legend has grown around the *Télémaque*, and three unsuccessful salvage attempts were made starting in 1837. In May 1939 the Entreprises Maritimes et Construction Navale, the company that won the bid, made a new attempt to salvage the wreck as it was obstructing navigation. The declared aim was to find the treasures. The raising of the front half of the ship took place on 3 April 1939, and the objects found inside were displayed at the Hôtel de la Marine in Quillebeuf.

The loot was meagre: fourteen silver coins, seven French and English gold coins, a gold necklace, as well as a dozen silver candlesticks, two bells, a large number of copper shoe buckles, watch winders, a sextant, copper organ pipes, balance weights, a set of locksmith tools, and timber that would be sold. It fell far short of covering the 2 million francs swallowed up in this affair. The German advance in the Second World War interrupted the salvage operation, and the stern of the *Télémaque* still lies at the bottom of the Seine. What became of the objects recovered from the wreck is unknown.

A painting behind the church altar is one of the rare representations of the old Quillebeuf lighthouse, established in 1817 and replaced in 1862 by the current lighthouse. It was this first lighthouse that served as a landmark to locate the wreck of the *Télémaque*.

AUCTION OF THE CANDLES

During the feast of St Gorgonius, girls choose melons and boys

Fête de Saint-Gorgon – Église Saint-Gorgon de Tocqueville
27500 Tocqueville
Information at Tocqueville town hall: 02 32 42 17 88
mairie.tocqueville@wanadoo.fr
Access via Bourneville (Normandie autoroute exit 26, then D139 towards Aizier, turn left towards Tocqueville)
The sale takes place in the cemetery, after Mass, around noon on first Sunday of September

St Gorgonius (or Gourgonius), a Roman officer in the palace of Diocletian, was martyred and torn apart in the 4th century for defending Christians. Invoked in several churches in Upper Normandy (see below), he's believed to relieve rheumatism and pains as well as help young children to walk. He's also invoked to find a spouse and overcome male impotence.

The discovery of male and female amulets made from enamelled glass paste, which were purchased during the 19th-century pilgrimage to the chapel of Saint-Gorgon in Genetey, Saint-Martin-Boscherville, leaves no doubt about the effect of his powers.

Once a year, on the first Sunday of September, the auction of candles at Tocqueville church during the feast of St Gorgonius is carried out in the same spirit. Each of the 13 statues of saints in the church is assigned a candle to be auctioned in the cemetery, in the presence of the Charitable Brotherhood. Until recently, St Gorgonius' candle was the largest. Although all candles are now the same size, that of Gorgonius is the most sought-after.

After the auction (which is done by weight of wax, with the price set each year in the church based on the market), the candles remain throughout the year and are lit at the foot of their assigned saint. The money collected is used to pay for the production of new candles for the statues in the church.

The ceremony is followed by a festival that used to bring together young people, where the famous melons from Marais Vernier, a type of squash no longer produced, were sold.

St Gorgonius is also invoked in Vironvay, Boissey-le-Chatel, Houetteville, Émanville and Fiquefleur in Eure region.

VOWS AT CHAPELLE SAINT-THOMAS

To heal rickets, malaria, or a marriage vow ...

Former medieval leper colony
27500 Aizier
*From Bourneville (Normandie autoroute exit 26), take direction Pont de
Brotonne, and after 600 metres continue straight towards Aizier (D139). In
village, follow signage (vehicle access via D95; pedestrian access 1.5-km walk
from centre of Aizier)*
*Free and open access throughout the year (discovery trail with explanatory
panels)*
*Guided tours for groups are available on reservation through Quillebeuf tourist
office at Bourneville; for more information: 02 32 57 32 23*

The chapel of St Thomas, whose Romanesque ruins lie in a particularly romantic site along the ancient Roman road from Lisieux to Lillebonne, protects the relics of a medieval leper colony. The site was occupied even before the Christian era, although the hospital was probably built only in the late 12th century. It was first documented in 1227, while the chapel was dedicated to St Thomas Becket, Archbishop of Canterbury, who was assassinated in his cathedral in 1170, canonised shortly after, and credited with numerous miracles. He became the object of significant cult worship in Normandy, particularly in the chapel at Aizier.

Thanks to recent studies on European leper colonies, we now know that these were communal spaces, much like a monastic institution with its own set of rules. The sick would come to do penance in order to be healed. From the 13th century onwards lepers were excluded from society, and colonies became reserved for the wealthy (typically around 10 stayed at Aizier). During the 16th century, St Thomas's lost its function as a hospital and became a priory dependent on Abbaye de Fécamp.

The pond next to the chapel was the focus of pagan veneration, later Christianised, expressed through tying knots round tree branches to cure rickets, as well as through pilgrimages and ablutions to seek relief from malarial fever. Since the 1950s couples have come to the chapel to make a marriage vow, tying a branch there, and returning one year later to see if the knot is still intact – guaranteeing a lasting marriage.

NEARBY
Chapelle Saint-Maur ⑨

Not far away, at St Maur's chapel in Brotonne forest, Vatteville-la-Rue commune, the saint is venerated (although there has been no statue of him there for several years) in the traces of a former hermitage. Branches were also tied to cure children unable to walk.

The overall improvement of people's sanitary arrangements and analysis of the little notes left on the altar as vows have made St Maur more 'versatile'. As with St Expeditus in Freneuse, emotional and material needs have largely taken precedence over those related to health and spirituality.

ORTIES FOLIES FESTIVAL

A piquant event

La Haye-de-Routot
Access to Routot via D686
The festival, which is combined with the Fête des Légumes Oubliés (Festival of Forgotten Vegetables), takes place in front of church, usually first Sunday of October
Organised by Roumois Terres Vivantes en Normandie association, Maison du Lin, Place du Général Leclerc, 27350 Routot
02 32 56 21 76
terresvivantes-normandie.fr
contact.terresvivantes@gmail.com

Orties Folies festival, launched at La Haye-de-Routot in 1995, once a year gathers all the nettle enthusiasts from France and beyond. A tent village is set up in this small commune of 265 residents, and over the course of a weekend a range of activities is offered. These include conferences, a gourmet market, exhibitions, food stalls, tastings, music and other entertainments all centred on the use of nettles and wild plants in gardening, cuisine, textiles, etc. The nettle is considered one of the most useful plants (see below).

In even-numbered years the festival expands to another region of France. Highly popular in La Haye-de-Routot, it attracts 3,000 to 4,000 visitors each year.

Multiple benefits of nettles

When used as a brew, nettle plants can act as a preventive insecticide, a tonic, or even a herbicide, depending on the dilution. When cooked, nettles are considered an extremely invigorating vegetable, and cooking removes the 'venom'.

For a long time nettle stems used to be retted (fibre separated from stem) and processed, just like flax and hemp, to obtain fibre and fabric known locally as lin gris (grey linen).

As dried forage for sheep, horses or goats, nettles are proven to be an excellent nutritional supplement.

For human consumption, nettles can be used in soup, tea, powdered on food, as syrup, or in various culinary preparations. They always provide a boost of vitality, which can also be experienced through flagellation with a bunch of nettles to stimulate circulation ...

TWO ANCIENT YEWS
AT LA HAYE-DE-ROUTOT

In 1865, 10 musicians played inside one of the tree trunks without getting in each other's way

27350 La Haye-de-Routot
La Haye-de-Routot is on southern edge of Brotonne forest
Trees in cemetery next to church
Free and open access to visitors

The two gigantic yew trees in La Haye-de-Routot, trunk circumferences 14 and 16 metres respectively, are estimated to be around 1,600 years old. So they were 'born' in the 5th century! In the 13th century the church and cemetery were built near these already imposing yews (see below). As the trunks of the ancient trees hollowed out over the centuries, the cavities became so large that in the 19th century the villagers decided to make use of them. A local newspaper reported in 1865 that 40 people stood together inside the larger yew, and a 10-piece band played without getting in each other's way

In 1866 the larger yew received a chapel dedicated to St Anne. In 1897 the other yew, with its cavity resembling Lourdes grotto (made famous by the apparitions of Bernadette Soubirous in 1858), received an oratory dedicated to Our Lady of Lourdes. And in 2001 the commune was awarded the 'Remarkable Tree' label for taking such care of the yews. It's worth noting that a clone of these age-old trees was raised in vitro by the Museum National d'Histoire Naturelle in Paris and replanted in the cemetery in 2007 to ensure their preservation into the next millennium.

NEARBY
Bouquetot hawthorn
On Rue de la Belle Épine, alongside the cemetery in Bouquetot, 8 km from La Haye-de-Routot, a 600-year-old hawthorn tree is lovingly maintained.

The yew, a tree both toxic and beneficial
Yews, capable of living for several centuries, soon became symbols of immortality so were often planted in cemeteries. Their foliage is toxic to domestic animals, discouraging them from wandering around and disturbing the eternal rest of the deceased.

Yews were also used in the Middle Ages for the elasticity and strength of their wood, which made them ideal for making war bows.

The arrows, made from ash wood, were also dipped in taxine, a toxic substance extracted from yew leaves that paralyses the muscles. The red casing of the yew seed is however harmless and eaten by some birds, so helping the tree to reproduce.

A molecule found in young yew shoots, taxotere, is now of interest to laboratories for treating certain cancers. The shoots are carefully cut each year for this purpose.

SAINT-CLAIR BONFIRE AT LA HAYE-DE-ROUTOT

Protection against lightning

27350 La Haye-de-Routot
Facing yew trees, on paved platform
Night of 16 July, starting 8pm
Contact: Jacky Bordeaux, President of Festival Committee: 06 60 26 87 04
Free parking available

The Saint-Clair bonfire at La Haye-de-Routot is a veritable institution that follows a codified ritual dating back centuries. Eight days before the feast of Corpus Christi, the 15 members of the Charitable Brotherhood fell a poplar tree. The following week the tree is split, cut and chopped by hand, following measurements in feet and inches that predate the French Revolution. The wood is then stacked in the cemetery to dry.

On 16 July at 6am the building of the pyre begins, entirely by hand and using no nails. The brothers, also known as *charitons*, and the festival committee gather on the ladder used to build this 15-metre-high wooden pyramid topped with a flower-covered wooden cross. The pyre must be completed by midday.

In the evening, after a folkloric parade followed by a procession of the *charitons* and a Mass, everyone follows the priest. After blessing the bonfire, the priest hands the lit Saint-Clair candle to selected individuals (a sought-after honour) to light the fire. When the flames have died down you have to retrieve a charred piece of wood, known as a *brandon*, and set it above your fireplace as protection against lightning.

According to another tradition, if the cross of the Saint-Clair bonfire burns, a war or other catastrophe will occur within the year. This often comes true, but the cross rarely catches fire ...

St Clair, a Welsh hermit who lived in the 6th century, supposedly left Wales under pressure from a princess with romantic designs on him. He crossed the Channel to settle in the Cherbourg region. His fame soon grew because of the miracles he performed as he journeyed on to the east of Normandy, leaving hermitages and places of worship along the way. He eventually arrived at what is now the village of Saint-Clair-sur-Epte, where he founded another hermitage. But two soldiers sent after him by the princess found and beheaded him. Even after beheading he allegedly performed a final miracle by holding his own head in his hands and walking on. He is worshipped for the restoration of sight.

The Charitable Brotherhoods, of which there are around a hundred in Eure department, consist of lay brothers responsible for burying the parish deceased and being charitable and devoted to their fellow humans.

STONE MILL
AT HAUVILLE

A technological innovation from the 13th century

27350 Hauville
Access via D315 between Bourg-Achard and La Mailleraye-sur-Seine and D101
towards Hauville
02 32 56 57 32 – moulinavent27@gmail.com
May–mid-Sept, Sunday afternoons and every afternoon during summer
holidays

Hauville windmill, known as the stone mill, whose presence is documented as early as 1258 although it was probably built 30 years earlier, owes its existence to Abbaye de Jumièges, which owned the mill until the Revolution.

The abbey required all farmers to grind the cereals produced on its land in its mills, in exchange for a fee. Considering the very early construction date of the stone mill and the archaeological and historical research carried out on the structure, it seems that the abbey experimented with the windmill as a technological innovation in Hauville. Windmills had been imported to the West 50 years earlier, on the way back from the Crusades.

The main advantage of wind over water mills is the possibility of reducing cereal transport, as the mill stands on the plateau where the wind blows, but also where the cereals are produced. The water mill, which is older and has been around since Roman times, allows energy to be stored in the form of water. Wind power could not be stored back then.

The stone mill is also the oldest and the only windmill to be restored to working order in Upper Normandy. Originally built on flat ground, the mill was destroyed during the Hundred Years' War and rebuilt in the same location, on a mound, in the 16th century. It was again destroyed in 1592 during the Wars of Religion between French Catholics and Protestants, then rebuilt and extended with an additional floor. It seems to have been completed in 1672, but as the original stones had partially disappeared, flint was used to fill the gaps. A thatched cottage was built nearby later in the 17th century, complemented by an oven and garden in the 18th century.

The mill's activities ended around 1880 and it was converted into an agricultural building. During the Second World War it was strafed and left abandoned. Restored in 1985 by the Parc Naturel Régional Boucles de la Seine Normande, it became a working museum.

CHAPELLE DE LA RONCE

Statue of the Virgin Mary that returns to its place in an oak tree

27310 Bas-Caumont
02 35 18 03 22
Take RD64 then RD93, 4 km from La Bouille along Seine riverbank at location known as La Ronce
Chapel can be reached via old quarry road once used to transport stone blocks from nearby quarry down to the Seine
Open during Heritage Days and pilgrimage, last Wednesday morning of May

The setting in which the story of La Ronce chapel unfolds is filled with mystery – along the banks of the Seine, at the foot of a cliff riddled with caves from which 'Caumont' stone has been extracted for centuries. One of the qualities of this stone is its resistance to freezing, making it a preferred choice for building beautiful houses, churches and monuments such as Rouen cathedral.

Sometime before 1843, lumberjacks tasked with felling trees in La Ronce woods noticed a small statue of the Virgin Mary embedded in the trunk of an oak tree. They cleared the area around the tree a little, removed the statue, and set it down nearby. As night fell, they returned home. To their astonishment, the next morning the statue of the Virgin Mary had 'returned' to its original spot in the oak tree. The landowners, called to witness the miracle, vowed to build a chapel by the tree, which would be consecrated in 1843 as Chapelle Sainte-Marie Mère de Dieu (Saint Mary Mother of God).

From its construction until 1972, the chapel became a pilgrimage site for neighbouring villagers, who would gather there every year on the last Thursday of May. The procession of around 150 people started from the church at Caumont-Haut, followed the Cavée (a narrow road that descends towards Caumont-Bas through a break in the cliff), then continued for several kilometres alongside the Seine to reach the chapel. A man from La Ronce even ferried pilgrims to the other side of the river in his boat.

In recent years the pilgrimage has been reduced to a Mass held inside the chapel for pilgrims from both sides of the Seine, and the grand procession from Caumont church has been abandoned due to the dangers of road traffic. The pilgrimage was however revived in 2008, now taking place on the last Wednesday of May with a short procession from the Seine quay.

BRIDGE TOWPATH WINDOW
AT ÉGLISE NOTRE-DAME-DES-ARTS

Challenges of navigation on the Seine

Église Notre-Dame-des-Arts
27340 Pont-de-l'Arche
Stained glass known as the 'towpath' on second window of right-hand aisle

The Pont de l'Arche was the first bridge built over the Seine in 862, long before the bridge at Rouen. It was commissioned by Charles the Bald (Charles II) with the dual aim of facilitating the river crossing near his home in Pitres and blocking the route to Paris in case of need to prevent Viking raids. The bridge was defended by gates that could be closed, putting a stop to any navigation.

The bridge is depicted in the *vitrail du halage* (towpath window) in Notre-Dame-des-Arts church at Pont-de-l'Arche, designed by Rouen artist Martin Vérel in 1605.

Reconstructed after the Treaty of Saint-Clair-sur-Epte in 911, which established Rollo as Duke of Normandy, the bridge has 23 arches, of which only three very narrow ones are open for navigation. It's fortified at both ends, to the north by the Château de Limaie and to the south by the ramparts of Pont-de-l'Arche.

At high tide it took no less than 200–300 men and 50–60 horses, under the orders of the bridge commander, to tow a boat under one of the bridge arches. Several hours were needed for this. But such manoeuvres proved lucrative for the towmen, who were paid through an official toll collected by the commander, and sometimes through an unofficial toll called '*chalannage*' (carnage), which supported part of the population.

Engravings from the 19th century show the arches cluttered with buildings, mills and fishing huts with drying nets. Due to this congestion as well as the water level, the passage was feared by bargees until 1813, when a lock was installed in the moats of the former Château de Limaie. The Martot dam, opened 7 km downstream in 1832, and the Poses dam, built 6 km upstream from Pont-de-l'Arche in 1885, made one of the most challenging stretches of the Seine navigable.

The famous bridge, now relocated 200 metres away, arose from the foot of Rue Alphonse Samain until the 1950s.

FAUVETTE TUGBOAT

Preserving the memory of inland navigation

64 Chemin du Halage
27740 Poses
02 32 59 08 44 or 02 32 61 02 13
Sundays and public holidays, 2.30pm–6pm May–end Oct
From Pont-de-l'Arche, take direction Poses (7 km) via D110. Park at dam and walk along towpath for 1.5 km to reach banks of the Seine

If one place evokes inland navigation on the Seine, in Normandy it has to be the village of Poses, where mariners often owned a little home from home facing the river. This is where they would rest during their rare breaks and where they would retire. This practice faded away with the massive mariner decline of the second half of the 20th century. The traditional stop-offs for these watermen, such as Amfreville-la-Mi-Voie and Harfleur in Seine-Maritime, also suffered. Only Conflans-Sainte-Honorine in Yvelines remains an important hub for boats on the Seine and its tributaries.

But there's a unique atmosphere in Poses, a sense of happiness and serenity. You don't notice the flowing river as the dam creates a calm lake. Along the towpath by the Seine, you'll soon discover the *Fauvette*, a tugboat classified as a Historic Monument, which can be visited.

Built in 1928 in Cologne, it was part of the fleet of the Compagnie des Oiseaux and, thanks to its 600-horsepower diesel engine, provided towing services on the Seine for strings of barges that could stretch for over a kilometre. The entire tugboat can be explored, from the captain's quarters to the engine room and wheelhouse.

A short distance upstream is the *Midway II*, a motorless barge like those once towed by the *Fauvette*, which houses the Musée de la Batellerie (Museum of Inland Navigation) and is also open to visitors. These two historic boats, preserved and lovingly restored by the Association des Anciens et Amis de la Batelleries de Poses, give an insight into on-board working and living conditions in the first half of the 20th century.

Another attraction not to be missed is the largest 'graffito' of a boat, over 3 metres long, on the exterior walls of the church in Poses. It represents a besogne (predecessor of the barge), as used on the Seine in the 19th century.

NEARBY
Fish observation chamber   (17)
Sundays and public holidays, 2pm–6.30pm May–Sept
Admission free

The impressive Poses dam, which has spanned the Seine since its construction in 1885, is accompanied by a set of locks on the right bank of the river in Amfreville-sous-les-Monts town. On the left bank, in Poses, a micro-power plant with four turbines was built in the 1990s. As required by law, the plant is equipped with a fish ladder. What makes this development unique is the installation of an observation chamber at a depth of 3 metres, so visitors can see the migrating fish as they swim up or down the river.

FORMER LEVAVASSEUR SPINNING MILL

A factory-cathedral unique in France

Fontaine-Guérard
From Pont Saint Pierre (27470), head towards Fleury-sur-Andelle via D321
Follow signs to Abbaye de Fontaine-Guérard via D714 and park in front of abbey
Site can be viewed from outside but closed to the public

The first mechanical spinning mill in the Andelle valley was installed in 1792 by François Guéroult. He drew inspiration from factories

operating in Britain under the supervision of an English engineer. The romantic setting of this old factory is such that many admiring visitors mistake it for the remains of the nearby Abbaye de Fontaine-Guérard.

After a difficult start, textile production exploded at the time of the French Empire thanks to protectionist policies, mechanisation, and Frenchwomen's enthusiasm for cotton fabrics.

In 1808 the mill employed 500 workers to spin cotton and merino wool and weave cloth. But British competition after the Bourbon Restoration in France brought about the ruin of the spinning mill. It was taken over by Jacques Levavasseur, a merchant-shipowner from Le Havre and founder of the cotton-spinning mill in Le Houlme, Seine-Inférieure (now Seine-Maritime) department, in 1816.

The site comprised five mills powered by the hydraulic force of the Andelle: three spinning mills (one for wool and two for cotton), a fulling mill and a wheat mill.

In 1845 a series of fires destroyed all these mills and Charles Levavasseur, the founder's son, set up a new establishment downstream from the site in 1851. It consisted of two buildings that would become a cathedral-like spinning mill unique in France.

The larger of the two neo-Gothic mills is 96 metres long and 36 metres tall. At the time it was one of the largest spinning mills in France, although it rarely operated at maximum capacity due to the cotton crisis. This had several causes: lack of local workforce (although the factory was designed for 600 workers, it rarely employed more than 150); competition from cheaper British cotton fabrics (30% cheaper) flooding the French market after the free trade agreement signed in 1860 between Britain and France; and the American Civil War, which reduced the exports of American cotton (raw material for the mill) to France. To adapt to the short fibres of Middle Eastern cotton, which replaced the American variety, new machinery had to be developed. One positive aspect of this crisis was that the shortage of American cotton revived the mechanical spinning of linen in France.

On 23 August 1874 the large wooden mill was engulfed in flames and completely destroyed overnight.

Nevertheless, spinning activity continued in the small mill, which was built at the same time as the large mill in the same style. Originally intended for weaving, it too fell victim to fire in 1913 and again in 1946, leading to the definitive abandonment of the site, which was subsequently sold off in parcels.

In 1974 Eure department acquired the entire ruins of the two mills, except for the hydroelectric power plant operated by Elbeuf municipal electricity board.

HEUDEBOUVILLE ROOF-RIDGE FINIALS

Familiar figures on the roofs

27400 Heudebouville
Village on D6015 between Gaillon and Louviers

To spot the ridge ornaments that crown the roofs of Heudebouville, walk through the alleys around the village church.

This village, with its traditional houses made from limestone rubble and roofs covered with small tiles, features numerous ridge ornaments representing human or animal figures. Among the humans you'll find Marianne (symbol of the French Republic), a priest, and especially mustachioed gendarmes with prominent sideburns. As for the animals, a cat and a dove are perched on different roofs.

The ones known as gendarmes are actually uniformed characters wearing medals on their chests and a metal plaque on a leather harness. They sometimes wear a shako military cap, sometimes a cocked hat, or even a kepi, which makes identifying them more complicated. You can't help but think of General Boulanger (1837–91), whose Boulangist 'movement' was in full swing in the late 19th century and made such an impact on people's minds. All the more likely as both the Musée de Normandie in Caen and the Musée des Traditions et Arts Normands in Martainville-Épreville have ridge ornaments from Heudebouville representing historical figures such as Dom Pedro II, Emperor of Brazil, who was overthrown by the Brazilian revolution in 1889 and lived in exile with his family at the Château d'Eu.

These ridge ornaments were probably made on-site in Heudebouville at one of the two brick and tile factories that, in the late 19th century, offered such roof decorations along with machine-made tiles. But the artist who designed them is unknown.

Ridge ornaments can also be found in nearby communities such as Ailly and Ingremare.

FONTAINE SAINTE-CATHERINE

Find a husband within a year

27440 Lisors
Take D715 from Lisors towards Lyons forest until you reach sources of the Fouillebroc, a small tributary of the Andelle. Pass by former Abbaye de Mortemer towards Lyons-la-Forêt. Fontaine Sainte-Catherine stands at edge of forest

St Catherine's fountain, one of the sources of the Fouillebroc, has been renowned since the 18th century for young girls seeking a husband. It was restored in 1987 and is easily accessible from the road. Making a small offering (such as hairpins or a coin) may help grant the wish.

The current owner of nearby Abbaye de Mortemer understands this well. Several times a year, in March and November, she used to organise a singles fair in the former abbey, with a mandatory stop at the 'Fountain of Singles', a 12th-century basin that collects water from St Catherine's chapel 1.5 km upstream.

This one-day event, unique in the region, was reserved for widowed or divorced singles of both sexes who badly wanted to start a family and establish new relationships. The seriousness of the candidates and the results were said to be excellent. But the singles fair has declined with the widespread use of the internet.

NEARBY
A spring to calm unbearable wives

In Les Hogues, 6 km from Lyons-la-Forêt towards Vascœuil, near the town hall, a spring called Saint-Mathurin used to be the objective of a pilgrimage. St Mathurin is believed to cure the mentally ill and have a calming effect on the possessed and on unbearable wives.

If someone makes a wrong choice with St Catherine, they can turn to St Mathurin to fix it!

A pilgrimage still takes place in Larchamp, Seine-et-Marne, where St Mathurin's relics are kept.

LEGENDS OF ABBAYE DE MORTEMER

Mortemer, the mother who dies a secular death to be reborn to spiritual life

Abbaye de Mortemer
27440 Lisors
02 32 49 54 34
abbaye-de-mortemer.fr/en/actualites-abbaye-de-mortemer.html
Daily 11am–6pm
Museum of tales and legends: daily 1 May–1 Sept 2.30pm–5.30pm
Nuits des fantômes organised Aug and Sept

Mortemer abbey was founded in 1134 under the patronage of King Henry Beauclerc of England (Henry I). It was the first religious house of the Cistercian order in Normandy, which itself was protected by the Knights Templar. Around 50 monks lived here in complete austerity, sustaining themselves with agricultural produce from the lands they owned around the monastery. The most famous among them was writer Philippe d'Alcripe (1531–81), known for his work *La Nouvelle fabrique des excellents traits de vérité* (The new workshop of excellent traits of truth). By the time of the French Revolution in the late 17th century the abbey was already in decline, with only four monks remaining. The revolutionaries sold the building as national property after persecuting and murdering the clerics, accusing them of conspiring against the people. It changed hands several times until the current owner founded a museum dedicated to the life of Cistercian monks in 1985.

There are many legends surrounding Mortemer, such as that of the '*garrache*' she-wolf. It's said that on the night of 1 January 1884, tenant farmer Roger Saboureau was hunting in Lyons forest around the Mortemer estate when he suddenly saw two eyes intensely staring at him. He then saw a huge wolf appear. Scared out of his wits, he shot and killed the animal. The next morning he was horrified to discover the bloodied corpse of his wife. He'd killed a '*garrache*', a cursed woman who roamed the countryside at the full moon as punishment for her sins. She was condemned to turn into a she-wolf seven times in seven villages around Mortemer abbey. This legend suggests that the model of virtue and sanctity encouraged by monastic life was a path for the people to follow to atone for their sins. The she-wolf is sometimes also conflated with the Capitoline Wolf from the legend of the founding of Rome, representing the Roman Catholic Church. The Cistercians didn't always have the best spiritual relations with Catholics, being offended by the luxury and pomp shown by the popes and their entourage. For example, the Cistercian saint Bernard of Clairvaux strongly criticised the sins of pride and opulence that dominated the Church. The Templars, whose rule was derived from this saint, sided with him, which greatly displeased the papacy.

Another legend speaks of the 'Goblin cat' (in Norman dialect: '*eul cat Goublin*'), a gnome that takes on the appearance of a cat and guards the abbey treasure in underground passages. Stray cats are often seen among the ruins, but it's impossible to follow them on a treasure hunt. The real Cistercian treasure lies in the Latin phrase *ora et labora* (pray and work), which represents spiritual exercise and intellectual and physical labour. Through its agriculture and stock-raising the Order bequeathed Mortemer with the treasures of spiritual life, intellectual creation and material prosperity, stimulating the socio-economic development of the region. Additionally, 'Goblin' is a distortion of the term *Gob* or *Gobi*, king

of the gnomes (elemental beings of the earth who live in or near caves and shy away from human contact). Because of this occult aspect the figure of the cat has been added, as a lunar and nocturnal animal whose feline nature accepts human presence as the mood takes it.

In the abbey museum, the 12th-century basin where the monks washed before dining is known as the 'Fountain of Singles'. It's said that if marriageable girls looking for a husband sprinkle their hair with this water, they'll find a husband within the year. The fact is that this often happened, which is why every year on the feast of St Catherine a large number of young girls come to wet their hair in the miraculous fountain. Symbolically, sprinkling the miraculous water on the hair is a sign of mental regeneration and physical strengthening, making it possible to marry after a life of chastity and purity.

Apart from the ghosts of the four monks murdered during the French Revolution, the ruins of Mortemer abbey are also haunted by the apparitions of the White Lady, Matilda of England (7 February 1102–10 August 1167), grandmother of Richard the Lionheart. Although legitimate heir to the throne of England and Empress of the Holy Roman Empire, her crown was claimed by her cousin Stephen of Blois in 1135 upon the death of King Henry I. This caused a civil war in England, known as 'Anarchy' because nobody understood what was happening anymore.

Retiring to the Norman lands, Matilda became the Countess of Anjou and Duchess of Normandy. She had been raised in the Cistercian abbey of Le Bec and maintained a close relationship with the Order throughout her life. She founded numerous Cistercian monasteries in England and Normandy and was the main benefactor and protector of Mortemer abbey, as seems to be confirmed by her apparitions. When she died, she was buried in front of the high altar of Le Bec abbey, but in 1846 her remains were transferred to Rouen cathedral. The White Lady is also an intrinsic part of the mythical heritage of the Templars (as well as Jewish, Greco-Roman and Celtic traditions), some of which has been passed down to the Cistercians. The White Lady represents the temporal aspect of the Divine Mother, the Universal Empress or Queen of the World. Clad entirely in white, like the Cistercians and Templars, she embodied the Living Purity of the Holy Spirit in its feminine form. This is also known in Judaism as Shekinah, which means 'the presence of God in the world'. Active in the community of believers, she acts upon their souls, making them whiter, in other words endowing them with the highest virtues.

MYSTERIOUS GRAFFITI
OF THE PRISONER'S TOWER

Templar graffiti?

Château fort de Gisors
27140 Gisors

22

Built by the Dukes of Normandy in the 11th and 12th centuries to defend the Anglo-Norman power against the claims of the King of France, Gisors castle was the site of the meeting in 1158 between English sovereign Henry II Plantagenet and King Louis VII to seal the reconciliation between the two kingdoms. The French sovereign then promised the hand of his 6-month-old daughter, Marguerite of France, to the son of the English king and offered the castle of Gisors as part of her dowry.

To ensure that neither party took advantage of this arrangement before the marriage, the castle was handed over to the Order of the Templars (see p. 230) and three of its knights, Robert de Pirou, Tostes de Saint-Omer and Richard of Hastings, were appointed to maintain it.

Around 1160, Henry II finally ordered the celebration of the wedding (after a papal dispensation, given the age of the bride and groom: 2 and 5 years) to seize the castle and its region, but the Templars still maintained their diplomatic position as mediators between the parties.

On his return from the Third Crusade (1188), Richard the Lionheart, successor to Henry II, was held prisoner from December 1192 to 4 February 1194, in Dürnstein, Austria, following disputes with German Emperor Henry IV. Philip Augustus (Philip II of France) took advantage of this opportunity to seize Gisors castle in 1193 and made numerous changes, including building what would later be called the Tour du Prisonnier (Prisoner's Tower).

When Richard the Lionheart was released, he took up arms to reclaim his Norman fiefdom, but the two parties eventually signed the peace treaties of Vaudreuil and Issoudun. These were supplemented the following year by the Treaty of Gaillon, which placed the county of Vexin – and thus Gisors – under the authority of the French crown.

With its loss of strategic fortress status, Gisors castle was converted into a state prison where political prisoners were temporarily incarcerated before trial.

When on 13 October 1307 King Philip IV of France (Philip the Fair) arrested the Templars, this fortress became a detention centre for many of them, including Jacques de Molay, the Grand Master, Hugues de Pairaud, Geoffroy de Gonneville, preceptor of Poitou and Aquitaine, and Geoffroy de Charney, preceptor of Normandy. They were imprisoned in the cellar of the castle tower. In memory of Jacques de Molay, who was held there, it was henceforth known as the Prisoner's Tower.

Some also say that this name doesn't come from the detention of Jacques de Molay and his companions but from another more recent episode – that of the prisoner Nicolas Poulain, a surgeon in Île-de-France, who in 1587 denounced a conspiracy against King Henry III of the faction known as Les Seize (the Sixteen) in Paris.

Members of the Guise family involved in the plot, seeking revenge, arranged for Poulain to be arrested, imprisoned and forgotten in the tower.

To pass the time, the poor wretch allegedly drew a series of graffiti with religious motifs on the walls of his prison. He's said to be the true author of the mysterious inscriptions (including the letters N and P, his initials) that can still be seen on the lower floor of the tower, although nothing has been definitively proven.

Among the graffiti are the blazons of wealthy knights, reminiscent of the noble origin of many Templars, and here and there roughly drawn but easily identifiable Maltese crosses of the Order of the Temple.

The graffiti with their strong Greco-Byzantine feeling (perhaps due to the Eastern influence that characterised the Order of the Templars, which spent most of its life and activity in the Middle East), also depict scenes from the life of Jesus and his mother, John the Baptist baptising him, Mary holding the child in her arms, and a series of scenes from the Passion of Christ.

The scenes from the Passion could have a double meaning: besides the immediate reference to the crucifixion, they may also allude to the cult of the royal blood. This was supposedly collected by Joseph of Arimathea in the Holy Grail, which Byzantines called the *Kratter* and later became the Provençal word *Graal*.

This vessel of the Last Supper and the Passion of Christ was brought to the West by Arimathea himself (see *Bretagne Nord insolite et secrète* and *Secret Provence*, also published by Jonglez). But according to Légende dorée (*Golden Legend*), the 13th-century collection of stories of the saints by Jacobus de Voragine, the vessel was brought back to the East, to Jerusalem. It was discovered by the Templars in the underground ruins of the Temple of Solomon and brought back to Western Europe for good.

Myth or not, the Templars are known to have attached special value to the celebration of the Passion and the Easter Resurrection, and the Eucharistic chalice (shown in Gisors graffiti) was one of their main liturgical objects.

23

TEMPLAR SYMBOLS IN ÉGLISE SAINT-GERVAIS-ET-SAINT-PROTAIS

Occult initiation symbols

27140 Gisors

The construction of Saint-Gervais-et-Saint-Protais church in Gisors, consecrated by Pope Calixtus II in 1119, dates back to the time of the Templars and the brotherhoods of monk builders under their protection. The architecture of this remarkable monument is a synthesis of different styles, ranging from Flamboyant Gothic to Renaissance, as the church had numerous makeovers between the 12th and 16th centuries.

Since the mid-20th century the church has been associated with the esoteric tradition of the Templars, who as the legend goes hid a fabulous treasure sought by King Philip IV of France in an underground chamber.

There is indeed historical evidence of a chamber beneath the church, where a statue of St Catherine of Mount Sinai stood, as well as a network of tunnels aligned on a north-south axis, suggesting underground connections between Gisors castle and this church.

It was the Templars who elevated the twin saints Gervasius and Protasius, sons of St Vital and the blessed Valeria, to the rank of patron saints of Gisors. They lived alongside another pair of twin saints, Celse and Nazare. They were martyred in the year 57 CE by order of Emperor Nero (Anzio, 15 December 37–Rome, 9 June 68) because they refused to renounce their Christian faith and condemned Roman idolatry.

The presence of the twins refers to the dual meaning of the Christian religion as understood by the Templars: the orthodox, exoteric, or public belief (the written scriptures) and the unorthodox, esoteric, or private faith (the spirit of the scriptures). It was under the invocation of St Gervasius and St Protasius that Jean de Gisors (1133–1220), a vassal of the King of England, restored peace with the King of France in 1188 through direct diplomatic mediation by the Templars. The treaty was called the 'peace of the elm' because it was signed under an elm tree that still stands near the castle.

In the past, when similar agreements between the rulers of the two countries had been broken under the same tree, these failures were referred to as 'cutting down the elm'. In addition to its diplomatic meaning, the expression is also a nod to the trade guilds, especially carpenters and joiners, as elm was the wood most commonly used in the construction of Gisors castle and church. As for the 'cut', it indicates the separation of powers and the respective competences of the guilds of builders and the Order of the Temple, which protected and supported them. The unorthodox signs of the Templars' esoteric doctrine, carved in wood and stone between the 12th and 16th centuries, appear throughout the church.

Starting at the front entrance, you'll find the disquieting Latin phrase *Terribilis est locus iste* (Terrible is this place).

Here, 'terrible' carries the meaning of the fear we must have of Divine manifestation on Earth. The corresponding illustration depicts Jacob's dream with angels ascending and descending a ladder connecting heaven and Earth (Genesis 28:12), an episode that alludes to the spiritual enlightenment reserved for the few. This celestial ladder is replaced in the church by the Tree of Jesse, father of King David, depicting the ancestors of Jesus.

The angels are repeated on the vault and columns of the church: they signify that this temple was constructed according to esoteric knowledge, forbidden to common mortals, in accordance with sacred geometry and architecture. These angels resemble cherubs (kerub in Hebrew), a word that means 'treasure', and alludes to both the heavenly treasure in the form of divine wisdom on Earth and the legendary treasure of the Templars.

Continuing through the church, the Column of Tanners is decorated with numerous scenes of their guild, some with a 'craft initiation' character. You can see a master tanner, staff in hand, with the word MARIA (patron saint of the Royal Art, depicted on a column by two architects opening a book and, beside them, a king). This is immediately followed by another column marked I S Z G, most likely the initials of the master stonemason of the Renaissance who carved it.

The Column of Dolphins, funded by the Royal and Military Order of Saint Louis, represents royal power through dolphins and fleur-de-lis. It also alludes to the divine kingship that began with Clovis, directly enlightened by the Holy Spirit revealed to him (see *Secret Paris*, also published by Jonglez).

In Saint-Clair's chapel, dating from 1526, a recumbent effigy on the left bears a Latin phrase that translates: 'Whoever you are, you will be struck down by Death. Therefore, take heed, repent. I am what you will be, a pile of ashes. Pray for me.' Beyond physical death, this refers to traditional initiations in which the initiate always goes through a phase of dying in secular life before opening up to a new and higher life. This is the meaning of Saint-Clair (Holy Light), which evokes the Light of the Christic initiation whose sacred mysteries are present in this church.

Templar sites in Normandy

When the knight-monks of the Order of the Temple were arrested in France on the night of 13 October 1307, by order of Philip IV the Fair, Normandy was enjoying a period of calm after frequent Anglo-French military clashes and was therefore remarkably prosperous.

After the abolition of the Order by Pope Clement V at the Council of Vienne, which took place between 1311 and 1312 near Lyon, the Templars' real-estate assets (castles, churches, houses, lands, etc.) were transferred to the Order of St John of the Hospital, commonly known as the Hospitallers, who immediately took possession of them. This is why many buildings that belonged to the Templars display the double cross of the Hospitallers superimposed or next to the Templar cross.

Accessible documents refer to the range of properties belonging to the Order of the Temple: forests, farms, mills, chapels, hospitals, etc. In addition to the castle and church of Gisors (see p. 218), there are several other monumental and historical relics of Templar presence in Normandy. For example, the Biochet-Bréchot museum in Caudebec-en-Caux occupies the oldest civil building in Normandy, still known today as Maison des Templiers (House of the Templars, photo opposite). This magnificent 13th-century construction was built to accommodate the monks of Saint-Wandrille (5 km away), who enjoyed the direct protection of the Templar knights. The building has some surprising features of medieval construction art, and Norman archaeological remains fill the museum.

Between 1123 and 1125, the Knights Templar founded the commandery of Valcanville at the request of Anglo-Norman King Henry I Beauclerc, according to a letter dated 1213 (Archives Nationales, MM 1092, No. 37), confirmed by the document of donation to the commandery (Archives Nationales, S 5466) established by Guillaume, Bishop of Coutances. This indicates that Lord Hugues d'Agre granted the church of Valcanville, its patronage, and all its rights to the Order of the Temple, which would henceforth be called Notre-Dame du Temple (the church is now dedicated to St Firmin).

There are still some remains of this powerful commandery, which occupied a vast domain: several chimneys and thick walls flanked by arrow slits. These ruins are now on private property, but the owners deserve credit for encouraging visitors.

Of the former Bretteville-le-Rabet (formerly known as La Rabelle), founded in 1154 and governed by the bailiffs of Caen and Alençon, only the heavily damaged parish church remains, but it still has some details dating back to the 12th and 13th centuries. These include the interesting sundial of St Alban and the medieval tower, which probably also dates from the time of the Templars.

In Baugy, about 16 km south-east of Bayeux and 20 km north-west of Saint-Lô, two towns that were former Templar possessions, a commandery was founded in 1148 by Roger Bacon III. There are still parts of the original chapel dedicated to Our Lady of the Temple, as well as the foundations of the manor house.

Originally the chapel consisted of a nave with five vaults. The building's austere appearance, flanked by massive buttresses, detracts from the elegance and simplicity it once possessed. At the west end the tympanum over a 13th-century door depicts a lamb carrying a Templar cross. This former commandery is now private property, but the owners welcome visitors on reservation.

In Courval or Corval, 4 km east of Vassy, is a place called Hospital (no doubt because of the Order of Hospitallers). There you can see the buildings of the former Templar commandery founded in June 1226 by Guillaume d'Aquila, preceptor of the Temple houses in Normandy, after an agreement with local seigneurial and ecclesiastical authorities. This is also private property, but is open to visitors. The commander's house is a 15th-century reconstruction, already from the time of the Hospitallers. The chapel, classified as a Historic Monument on 2 September 1994, is a mid-12th-century construction and still retains some fragments of sculptures and frescoes.

There is historical evidence of the establishment of a Templar commandery at Louvigny (Calvados) in the 13th century, but it was so poor that it could provide for only one knight, Guy Pasnaye. The town's church, dedicated to St Vigor, dates from the 14th century. It retains some symbolic elements that can be attributed to the Templars, ranging from a shining cross to a pilgrim angel. At Caen you can visit the ruins of St Julian's parish church, which dates back to the 7th century and has been rebuilt many times. The church belonged to the Templars in the 12th century and was first referenced in 1150. It was then part of the Voismer Templar commandery at Fontaine-le-Pin.

When the Order of the Temple was abolished at the beginning of the 14th century, St Julian's was given to the Hospitallers. Because of the patronage of Saint-Julien l'Hospitalier, the title of pastor commander (or 'souls' guide') was attributed to the prior of St Julian's. The ceremonies of enthronement to the Order of St John of the Hospital (later of Malta) of new knights from Caen were also held in this church. Also in Caen, some of the symbols in St Peter's church recall the unorthodox chivalrous tradition of the Templars. For example, the 'Arthurian' knight Lancelot of the Lake is shown crouched on the magical 'sword in the stone' Excalibur or Caliburn, his bridge between the Celtic tradition (represented by a kind of marine dragon) and Christianity (represented by a lion supporting the blade tip).

Templar relics are rare and scattered at the commandery of Saint-Vincent-des-Bois, founded in 1231 by the commander of the Templars of Bourgoult, since 1219 at Harquency in the commune of Andelys. But in Val-de-la-Haye are the remains of the former commandery of Saint-Vaubourg, which then belonged to the Hospitallers.

The castle and church of Saint-Jean-Baptiste are contemporaries of the Templars, but they have lost their authenticity through successive modifications.

There remains the Templar commandery of Villedieu-la-Montagne with its old chapel, now the parish church of Villedieu. Its hexagonal tower and some architectural features of the original building are well preserved.

Knights Templar: myths and reality

The Poor Knights of Christ and of the Temple of Solomon (Latin: *Pauperes Commilitones Christi Templique Salomonici*), better known as the Order of the Templars or the Knights Templar, was the best-known religious and military order of the Middle Ages. Founded on the return from the First Crusade in 1096, with the apparent purpose of protecting Christians who wished to make a pilgrimage to Jerusalem, the Order existed for nearly two centuries.

The Templars, officially endorsed by Pope Honorius II in January 1128, soon became the preferred charitable order throughout Christendom. Growth was rapid, both in terms of membership and power. The Knights Templar, dressed in their distinctive white mantles (because they followed the Rule of Cluny, Cistercian) with the red pattee cross, were the most skilled combat units in the Crusades. The non-combatant members of the Order managed a vast economic structure (they pioneered the letter of credit, precursor to the modern banking system) and erected numerous fortresses and temples across Europe and the Holy Land.

The magnificent organisation of the Templars had a dual purpose: the establishment of what could be called the United States of Europe today, together with public education, mandatory and free, but Templar and non-secular.

The Order therefore operated on two levels: the external and visible, and the internal or esoteric. The secular section consisted of men of action, dynamic and military, while the initiatic section was the true elite, the wise and priests in the rearguard of the knights and warriors. Both factions answered only to the Grand Master, not to kings or the pope, which led to suspicions of heresy even though they were merely exercising obedience. The Templars were also thought to practise heretical cults due to the secrecy of their ceremonies, but this was never verified because 'civilians do not enter military houses'.

The Order was strictly Roman Catholic and apostolic, apart from the intellectual interest of some of its members in other cultures and theologies, particularly Gnosticism, whose symbols occasionally marked their temples and castles. St Bernard of Clairvaux, spiritual mentor of the Templar Order, initially selected nine members from the elite group of distinguished initiates and sent them to Jerusalem, where King Baldwin II allowed them to settle in the underground stables of the ruins of the Temple of Solomon. According to certain secret traditions, it was there that they supposedly found the chalice of Solomon, lost or hidden since the time of Jesus Christ (the famous Holy Grail). They are said to have brought it back to the West, from which point its domination spread all over the world with the rapid rise of the Order.

Following the loss of the Holy Land, the support of European monarchies for the Templar Order diminished. King Philip IV of France, who had incurred a significant debt with the Order and had no means of repaying it, began pressuring Pope Clement V to take action against the Templars.

False evidence was fabricated and rumours spread, both about their sexuality and the sincerity of their faith. They were claimed to worship a bizarre and demonic figure called 'Baphomet', whose true identity was never known but was, in fact, a pure invention. In 1307, a great number of the Templars in France were arrested and tortured to the point of making false confessions. They were burned at the stake or condemned to the galleys. On 22 March 1312, under constant pressure from King Philip, Pope Clement abolished the Order.

In Portugal, the Templars were considered innocent by the king Dom Dinis, and many who had fled from France received immediate protection there.

Once the Order was dissolved, the Portuguese king immediately established another order in which former Templars could integrate: the Military Order of Our Lord Jesus Christ, or the Order of Christ.

The sudden disappearance of the majority of the Templars' European infrastructure gave rise to speculations and more or less exotic legends.

The cross of Neauphle Saint-Martin (12th century), along the D10 near Gisors, is attributed to the Templars.

CHÂTEAU DE BIZY
PEDILUVIUM

24

A *historic* pool for washing horses

27200 Vernon
02 32 51 00 82
chateaudebizy@gmail.com
chateaudebizy.com
20-min walk from Vernon train station

The gardens surrounding the remarkable Bizy castle offer a pleasant stroll of about an hour. It begins in the magnificent courtyard, closed off to the north by the former 18th-century stables. The lovely basin in the centre of the courtyard has a feature easily missed: a *pediluvium* (Latin for footbath), which means a pool used for washing horses, particularly after hunting with hounds.

Built in the 18th century at the request of the Duke of Belle-Île, grandson of Nicolas Fouquet, the *pediluvium* consists of a basin with a depth ranging from 130 cm to 170 cm and a ramp on either side for equestrian access.

Other pediluviums *in France*

Pediluviums were once quite common in villages and agricultural settings in France, although most have since been demolished. The best known today is probably the one at Marly-le-Roi, called the *abreuvoir de Marly*. The basin has a front without a rim so that horses can get in and out easily. The Marly watering trough was also used to rinse horse-drawn carriages, so that the entire team could be cleaned. Another survives at the Domaine de Villarceaux (Val d'Oise).

RESTAURANT OF FORMER HÔTEL BAUDY

A prominent Impressionist site

81 Rue Claude Monet
27620 Giverny
02 32 21 10 03
Daily except Mon, 1 April–31 Oct

Discovered in 1886 by William Metcalf, one of the first American painters to settle in the Epte valley, the former grocery-bar run by Lucien and Angélina Baudy became the Hôtel Baudy in 1887. It mainly attracted Anglo-Saxon artists seeking inspiration near Claude Monet, and quickly became the centre of the American Impressionist colony. Several studios were set up there between 1885 and 1915.

Théodore Robinson, Théodore Wendel, John Leslie, Frédéric W. MacMonnies, Mary Cassatt, Breck, Théodore Butler (who married Monet's stepdaughter, Suzanne Hoschedé), and others stayed there. In 1896 Baudy's son, Gaston, took over the hotel management along with his wife, Clarisse, while its founder continued to be involved. They set out tennis courts, served English and American dishes, organised parties and balls, sold art supplies, and exhibited the paintings of the artists who frequented the place.

From 1890 onwards Claude Monet, annoyed by the invasion of the village by painters, retreated to his garden. Although the First World War slowed down interactions, Hôtel Baudy remained the social centre of the village until the Second World War.

The former hotel has now been converted into a restaurant-museum, thanks to the artwork left by the artists as payment for their lodgings or out of friendship. A magnificent rose garden embellishes the site.

Dining on the terrace during the day or by candlelight in the evening, sheltered by trellises covered with greenery, or in the 1900s-style dining rooms, is an undisguised pleasure for those who have taken the time to visit Monet's garden and house. There is also a new Musée des Impressionismes, which succeeded the Terra Foundation's American Museum of Art celebrating the American Impressionist artists' colony. The place has plenty of charm and serves reputable traditional cuisine.

The spirit of the artists and famous figures who came to this historic site (including Cezanne, Renoir, Sisley, Rodin and Clemenceau) to meet the master is still there, and you mustn't leave without a stroll through the rose garden up to the artist's studio. Built in 1887 for William Metcalf, it sits in its original state amidst winding paths lined with roses and perennial plants. Open to visitors.

PIERRE
DE SAINTE-RADEGONDE

Healer of skin diseases

27620 Giverny

The Pierre de Sainte-Radegonde (St Radegund's Stone), in the cemetery around Église Sainte-Radegonde near the war memorial in Giverny, refers to the remains of an ancient covered alley.

Often missed by visitors who come to see the graves of Claude Monet and his family or Gérald Van der Kemp – the chief curator of the Palace of Versailles who revived Monet's memory by having his house and garden repurchased by the Terra Foundation – this Neolithic stone and the remains of the two supporting pillars are of historical significance.

This monumental stone, also known as St Radegund's tomb, is regularly worshipped. People rub against it or lie on it in order to seek cures for skin diseases such as scabies, eczema or leprosy.

This practice is associated with St Radegund, a 6th-century Germanic princess who was forced to marry Clotaire I, one of the sons of the Frankish king Clovis. Instead of leading the worldly life of a queen, Radegund dedicated herself to helping the sick and lepers.

She founded Abbaye Sainte-Croix at Poitiers, which no longer exists but was the resting place of her relics. Her official tomb is a Merovingian sarcophagus in the crypt of Église Sainte-Radegonde, also at Poitiers.

NEARBY
Dampsmesnil covered alley ㉗

The world's first documented archaeological discovery of a covered alley under a tumulus, containing an ossuary of 20 individuals, was in 1685 at Cocherel, 15 km to the south in the Eure valley. Although the site is no longer to be seen, you can visit Dampsmesnil (15 km north of Giverny, towards Magny).

It features a burial chamber consisting of three dolmens, notable for the depiction of a goddess of death with necklaces on her exposed chest, symbolised by two breasts.

MUSÉE DES INSTRUMENTS À VENT 28

The French birthplace of wooden wind instruments

Near church, 27750 La Couture-Boussey
02 32 36 28 80 – musee@lacoutureboussey.com
Open Tues–Sun 2pm–6pm
Closed 1 May and 16 Nov–31 Jan
5 km from Ivry-la-Bataille via D833 towards Saint-André-de-l'Eure

In France, La Couture-Boussey has the same reputation for wooden wind instruments as the town of Mirecourt has for string instruments and Tulle for accordions. The French musical instrument industry was born in La Couture-Boussey in the late 16th century because local boxwood was already being worked by woodturners. Starting in the late 17th century, Jacques Martin Hotteterre, from a dynasty of instrument manufacturers, put the town on the map by producing wind instruments that were first played at the nearby Château d'Anet and later at Versailles and other European courts. In the early 19th century the popularity of brass bands and orchestras led to mass production and a worldwide export trade that lasted until the 1970s–80s. But traditional production methods, carried out in family workshops and sometimes at home, were severely affected by Asian competition.

There is now only one local company manufacturing oboes, while two others specialise in producing high-end accessories for professionals. The Museum of Wind Instruments was founded in 1888 by the finishing workers who formed a union with the aim of preserving the history of their industry, patents, and the craftsmanship of traditional instruments, as well as providing professional training. The collections have been maintained by the town hall, and the original display cases are still in use.

Since it opened the museum has expanded to include collections of wind instruments from the 18th century to the present, representing

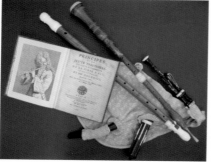

various woodwind instruments such as flutes, clarinets, oboes, Baroque court musettes, galoubets (type of flute), English horns, etc. The museum also features machines and workstations used in the production process and now plans to launch a sensory experience of music.

CHÂTEAU D'IVRY-LA-BATAILLE

The keep that inspired the Tower of London?

Access via D836 or D143 between Pacy-sur-Eure and Dreux, through Eure valley Park at foot of Église Saint-Martin and walk up to castle
Admission free

The donjon or keep of Ivry-la-Bataille castle, attributed to an architect named Lanfred and believed to have been built shortly before the year 1000, is considered one of the earliest and most monumental Norman constructions to defend the border and control navigation on the Eure river. After the excavations and restoration work carried out on the castle, there only remains the base of the large rectangular keep with its herringbone masonry. Despite Lanfred's execution on the orders of Orderic Vitalis of Aubrée, the woman who commissioned the keep and wife of Rodulf d'Ivry, Count of Bayeux, to prevent him from replicating such a construction anywhere else, the Tower of London is thought to be

inspired by the Ivry keep. In the late 12th century, the castle's defence was strengthened with a rampart punctuated by towers, which have been beautifully uncovered through recent restoration work. The Hundred Years' War ultimately led to the fortress's demise, as it was dismantled in 1449 by military leader Jean d'Orléans, Count of Dunois.

NEARBY
Ivry obelisk

Located 7 km from Ivry-la-Bataille in Épieds commune, via D833 towards La Couture-Boussey, then direction Épieds (D163) – Free access

On 14 March 1590, during the French Wars of Religion, Henry IV achieved a decisive victory over the Catholic League forces commanded by the Duke of Mayenne. A monument was erected at the spot where the king rested after the battle. Restored in 1777 by the Duke of Penthièvre, Lord of Anet, it was destroyed during the Revolution and restored once again in 1804 by Napoleon Bonaparte. The stone obelisk with its commemorative plaques stands at the centre of a circle at the end of a driveway lined with majestic lime trees. This battle led to the town of Ivry taking the name Ivry-la-Bataille.

ÉGLISE DE SAINT-MARTIN STALLS

31

Initiatory symbolism of trade guilds

27320 Nonancourt
02 32 58 28 74 or contact Monsieur Guingnier: 06 21 10 19 98
Guided tours available on request at tourist office

Built in the early 12th century and reconstructed in 1205, St Martin's church in Nonancourt (whose bell tower is the main relic from that period) was restored in the 16th century. Its exceptional collection of stained-glass windows date from that period (1500–30), and the choir stalls are carved with small, surprisingly unorthodox grotesque figures. These include a crouching man staring fixedly at a monkey sitting absorbed in a book, and a devil with a wolf's body supporting a backrest with his arms outspread to form a triangle.

The stalls are the work of a 16th-century guild of master carpenters, and considering the significance of the sacred for workers' guilds (see p. 248), you'd naturally think that the first character is probably a master carpenter himself.

Carved in a crouching position, rear end in the air, he highlights a sacred part of the human body – the sacrum. Looking down towards the ground, he symbolically indicates something hidden, something below the surface. This was most likely the secret knowledge of the master carpenter, who was head of a traditional trade initiation that would have been part of early Freemasonry, where joiners, carpenters and masons worked together. The monkey reading a book is in accordance with

the Egyptian symbolism reserved for the god Thoth (same as the Greek Hermes), who sometimes appeared with a white monkey's head and was the patron of scholars and literati.

In his function as a divine scribe, he takes note of the word of Ptah, the creator god, which he transmits to humanity so that they may evolve along the divine path. The book that the monkey is attentively reading is probably the Book of Wisdom. While in Christian iconography the monkey is often the image of a man degraded by his vices, particularly lechery and wickedness, here it represents the opposite.

The book indicates the antithesis of immorality, as the wise man is the opposite of the sinner. The monkey also appears in Hindu iconography as the royal monkey Hanuman, representing the 'Buddha of Compassion' (Bodhisattva). Hanuman, born of heaven, suffering out of love for mankind on Earth, brings them his teachings and guides them towards their common destiny, superior and spiritual.

The devil with a wolf's body supporting the backrest is depicted on one knee. The wolf is the animal form traditionally used to designate those initiated into the secrets of knowledge that was diabolical (or awesome, as inaccessible to common mortals, which explains why people associated any knowledge they didn't understand with the devil), placed under the feminine patronage of Mary.

In ancient Egypt, initiates donned a golden wolf mask under the patronage of Isis and her mysteries. The initiates of Isis were called jackals or wolves.

The triangular shape of the carving indicates the three main trades of the Royal Art – geometry, architecture, carpentry – where the first designs, the second sculpts, and the last shapes the temple of the soul that accompanies physical enlightenment. In other words, the ideal and the material temple are constructed simultaneously.

The wolf, and its derivative the wolf cubs, is a designation chosen by Freemason Robert Baden-Powell, the founder of scouting, to refer to the younger scouts preparing to be initiated by the fraternity of other scouts.

WINDMILL
AT MESNIL D'ACON

32

An original and historic turbine

Mesnil d'Acon farm, 27570 Acon
Travelling on RN12, between Nonancourt and Tillières-sur-Avre, heading
towards Alençon, take D672 towards Mesnil d'Acon for 1 km. At first
roundabout, this windmill can be seen above farm buildings in an open yard
For more information: article by Marcel Caron published in Confluences 2019
catalogue by Association Monuments et Sites de l'Eure

The *éolienne Bollée* (Bollée windmill) at Mesnil d'Acon, near Tillières-sur-Avre, is apparently the last in Eure department, which once had up to 23 of them.

This machine, installed on the farm in 1892, is one of the oldest of that type. Its function was to pump up water for farm animals, as the water table at this site is 45 metres deep.

The originality of these windmills is that Ernest-Sylvain and August-Sylvain Bollée, in their first patent dating back to 1875, combined two wheels fitted with blades. One was static (a set of fixed blades or stator) and the other mobile (the rotor), as in turbines. The blades of the rotor and stator are curved in opposite directions to increase the horizontal flow of air.

In a further patent dated 1885, which covers the Mesnil d'Acon windmill, the Bollée brothers added a system that turns the turbine to face the wind. Furthermore, the pipe carrying the transmission mechanism is hollow and operates connecting rods that raise the water. It carries an attractive cast-iron plaque with the name of the manufacturer.

The elegance of these windmills is largely due to their 15-metre cast-iron column made in 2.85-metre sections, around each of which snakes a spiral staircase with 12 treads, allowing them to be built to any desired height.

The windmill reportedly stopped operating in the 1950s when the commune installed a water distribution system. In the shed at the foot of the turbine you can still see the pumps and water tank.

All the bearings were made from bronze to reduce friction and avoid the need for frequent greasing. Production of these windmills ended around 1920.

MUSÉE
DE L'ÉCORCHÉ D'ANATOMIE

A museum unique in the world

54 Avenue de la Libération
27110 Le Neubourg
02 32 35 93 95 – museum@le-neubourg.fr
Daily except Mon and Tues 2pm–6pm

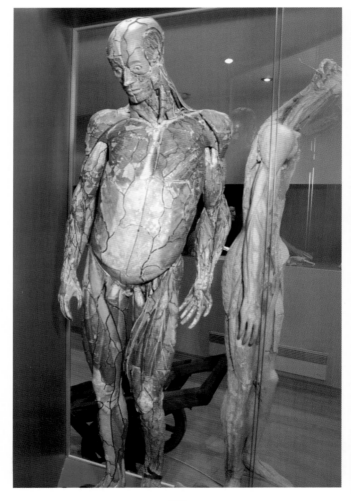

D r Auzoux. originally from Saint-Aubin-d'Écrosville, 8 km from Le Neubourg, studied medicine in Paris. To help medical students learn anatomy and faced with the difficulties of dissecting corpses due to the smell and the challenges of procuring or preserving them, he developed an artificial flayed human anatomical model consisting of 96 detachable organs, faithfully reproduced.

After five years of observation, certification and refinement, in 1828 he began mass-producing these models. The parts were made from a mixture of papier-mâché, clay, cork and glue, following a secret recipe. To expedite the manufacturing process, the organs were formed in wooden moulds covered with a lead alloy to shape the different parts. Then veins, arteries and nerves made from wire coated with paper and ribbon, and subsequently painted, were added. All the parts of the puzzle had to be removable so that future doctors could learn anatomy and the art of healing.

Success was assured and the Auzoux establishments employed over 50 workers in Saint-Aubin-d'Écrosville. Production diversified to the animal and plant world, as well as enlarged replicas of human organs (ear, kidney, heart …). Dr Auzoux distributed these anatomical models to medical schools, high schools and colleges worldwide.

At the end of the company's activity in 1980, the owner, Monsieur Barral, donated the tools and finished or partially assembled pieces to the town of Le Neubourg to create the extraordinary Anatomical Dissection Museum seen today.

OCCULT MARKS AND SYMBOLS AT ÉGLISE SAINT-PIERRE

The secrets of medieval operative Freemasonry

27250 Chéronvilliers

St Peter's church in Chéronvilliers, dating from the late 12th century, underwent restoration in the 16th century, during which its western and southern walls were rebuilt. From this period, a somewhat weathered group of three busts and two lions survive on the southern side door.

The lion, king of beasts, is also the astrological sign of the Sun, the king of celestial bodies. In the mineral realm, gold, the noblest of metals, represents the Sun. Thus the lion became a symbol of royalty

and medieval operative Freemasonry, once known as the Royal Art (see following double-page spread), which left numerous marks and symbols on the church walls. Next to the southern side door is a Gothic window topped with a coat of arms and two side medallions bearing the likeness of a noble, perhaps whoever commissioned this work in the 16th century. In the centre of the windowsill is an engraved band in the shape of a cross, which at the time meant 'I had it made, and so it is finished', closed or crossed out with a cross (completed).

On the western side door there's also a carved head of a master builder with horns, identifying him with the Devil. Advanced knowledge was forbidden to those uninitiated into the secrets of geometry and architecture.

The monastic brotherhoods of builder-monks and master stonecutters, who jealously guarded these secrets, were regarded as diabolical creatures possessed by supernatural secrets that no mortal could share. Beneath this carved head, the engraving of a tree with clover flowers emerging from an urn (a vase was set on top) is a veiled reference to the divine Tree of Paradise (divine prerogative was indicated by the three-leaf clover, representing the Holy Trinity). This model was used by medieval builders to establish the foundations of the structure to be erected. In Greek mythology, the urn signified divine providence (which oversees the construction work), while the sealed vase, as seen here, indicated the place where wonders occur (related to the hermetic art of the master builders).

On the same western side door, but on the opposite side of the cornice to the group described above, a pendulum terminating in a diamond-shaped cross (signifying the builder-monks as upright individuals and devout Christians) is positioned above a heart pierced by two crossed arrows in the shape of an X. This refers to the heart of Mary, patron saint of the Royal Art in the Middle Ages.

Within this sculpted heart are the letters S and M, probably the initials of the stonecutter's name and, of course, those of St Mary. Below the heart appears a craftsman's mark, identifying the master craftsman and the guild to which he belonged.

Operative Freemasonry and the Royal Art

Operative Freemasonry, formerly known as the Royal Art, derives its name from a legend that suggests Freemasons were initiated into sacred architecture and geometry while building Solomon's Temple in Jerusalem under the king's personal supervision. Hence the term Royal Art: the operative practice of this external initiatory process accompanied the mystical construction of the inner temple, making the initiate a 'King', a 'Master' of himself and of nature, exerting control through the sciences of architecture and geometry. In the Middle Ages, master masons and stonecutters built magnificent palaces and churches at the command of kings and princes of the Church, which once again justified the meaning of Royal Art. As alchemy is also referred to as the Royal Art, numerous alchemical symbols appear on buildings constructed according to the principles of sacred architecture. These symbols originated from one of three phases of Masonic evolution:

- Primitive Freemasonry, which concluded with the Collegia Fabrorum, Roman schools of artisan-artists founded around 500 BCE and disappearing around 400 CE.
- Operative Freemasonry, comprised of various craft guilds (surveyors, architects, masons, stonecutters, carpenters, etc.) that lasted from the early 5th century until 1523.
- Speculative Freemasonry, consisting of intellectuals who studied the ancient symbols of their predecessors, founded in 1717 and still in existence today.

Ancient brotherhoods of builders, including master masons and stonecutters, recognised each other through symbols and signs (marks of the labourers) that they inscribed on the surfaces of the buildings where they were working. Symbols were created in the masonry. These marks served not only to identify the individual

craftsman (a sort of personal monogram) but also his affiliated guild. They were unique symbols belonging to the symbolism of a collective. Some argue that the labourer's marks served the sole purpose of identifying him for payment. But this viewpoint is only partially correct, as most of the carved signs have been identified and belong to the heritage of mystical and esoteric symbolism.

Therefore they are sacred symbols. In the medieval era, when spiritual and religious intensity dominated society, it was highly unlikely that personal identification marks for payment purposes (profane reasons) would be engraved on religious buildings.

More plausibly, stone inscriptions correspond to the insignia of the companions' brotherhood, their seal on certain parts of their work. These marks express, in veiled or esoteric terms through the universal language of symbols, the essence of their doctrine.

Four main varieties of masonry marks can be distinguished, based on whether they are engraved on monuments or incunabula:

- Paleochristian marks (predating the Christian era);
- Kabbalistic magical marks;
- astrological marks;
- numerical marks.

At times these varieties are mixed, as seen in St Peter's church in Chéronvilliers (see previous double-page spread).

STATUE OF ST LOUIS

(35)

When 'St' Napoleon became St Louis ...

Église Sainte-Croix
Rue Thiers – town centre
27300 Bernay
Open daily morning–evening (exact hours available at tourist office)

The imposing statue of a man that sits on the left side of the choir in Bernay's beautiful Holy Cross church, built between the 14th and 19th centuries, is officially meant to represent St Louis (1214–70).

Astute observers will however notice some curious details: a bee near the tassel of the cloak, an eagle on the medallion worn on the chest, and most notably, a face that strikingly resembles that of Napoleon …

Indeed the statue, erected in 1813, was originally that of Napoleon Bonaparte in his imperial attire.

Abbot Lefebvre, the first priest appointed to the Holy Cross since the Revolution, had obtained permission from Cardinal E.H. de Cambacérès, following a decree issued in 1808 under Napoleon I, to acquire a share of the furnishings from the former abbey church of Bec-Hellouin (Eure), ravaged during the French Revolution.

The Revolution also expelled the last monk from Bec-Hellouin in 1792. Over the course of 10 years the buildings suffered various forms of degradation and looting: the library was pillaged, sculptures were smashed. In 1802 Napoleon converted Bec-Hellouin into a military horse stable, under the jurisdiction of the national stud Haras du Pin, thereby saving it from complete destruction. The religious furnishings (main altar, rood screen …) and the abbots' tombstones were transferred to Holy Cross church in Bernay, while the abbey church and chapter house were sold as a stone quarry in 1809. The riding school was set up in the 17th-century cloister, and the main stable in the refectory of the same period (now the abbey church).

To show gratitude to the government for allocating the assets of Bec Hellouin to the church, Abbot Lefebvre had a statue of Napoleon Bonaparte erected there in 1813.

A few years later, during the Restoration of 1814–30, 'St' Napoleon was opportunistically turned into St Louis, in that the bees on his cloak were replaced with fleurs-de-lis. But the face still fails to deceive experts on the former emperor.

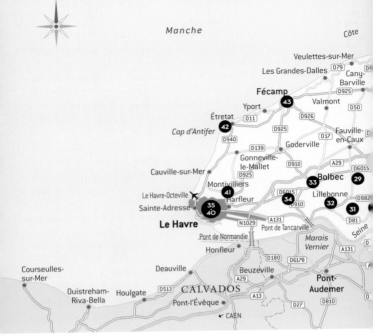

Seine-Maritime

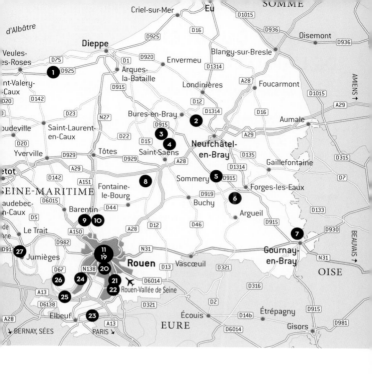

FESTIVAL DU LIN ET DE L'AIGUILLE

Flax, the star crop of Cauchoise agriculture

Association Alliance et Culture
6 Rue Louis Pasteur – 76740 Fontaine-le-Dun
02 35 57 25 20
allianceetculture@wanadoo.fr
festivaldulin.org
Every year, beginning of July

The Linen and Needle Festival event takes place over three days in eight municipalities of the Dun valley and surrounding plateau (Sotteville-sur-Mer, Saint-Aubin-sur-Mer, Le Bourg-Dun, Saint-Pierre-le-Vieux, La Gaillarde, Saint-Pierre-le-Viger, Fontaine-le-Dun, Angiens). Organised every year in early July by the Alliance et Culture association, the festival's mission is to promote flax, the star crop of Cauchois agriculture.

The festival offers exhibitions of patchwork and embroidery, a linen market with over 50 exhibitors from all over France, and various

activities including workshops and classes for adults and juniors, visits to linen-processing factories, linen-themed hikes, and fashion shows featuring talented designers.

Upper Normandy is the leading linen-producing region in France (40,000 hectares cultivated, accounting for 50% of the country's linen-growing areas). With 15% of their agricultural land dedicated to flax cultivation, the coastal districts of Fontaine-le-Dun – where the Linen and Needle Festival takes place – and Saint-Valery-en-Caux hold the national record for linen production.

Linen has left its mark on the history of the Pays de Caux and still shapes the landscapes from spring to autumn. It remains an environmentally friendly natural fibre with proven dermatological benefits dating back thousands of years.

The by-products of linen production are also used in the manufacturing of industrial composite materials such as ropes, paper, horse bedding and horticultural mulch.

Flax is primarily known for its textile uses, which have been established for over 5,000 years. New applications for this exceptional fibre, including as a replacement for carbon fibre, are currently being studied.

NEF VÉGÉTALE VESSEL

Clay in light and shade

Château de Mesnières-en-Bray park
Lycée Horticole et Silvicole– Institution Saint-Joseph
76270 Mesnières-en-Bray
02 35 93 10 04 (accommodation and catering on reservation)
chateaudemesnieres.reservation@gmail.com – chateau-mesnieres-76.com
Daily 2.30pm–6.30pm, 1 July–31 Aug, except Tuesdays and certain holidays
Guided tour of castle: 45 min
Groups welcome throughout the year on reservation

A sort of large fish covered in glazed stoneware scales floats in a basin among its lively counterparts. This amazing monumental sculpture, topped with a mast, stands in the courtyard of the Horticultural and Forestry High School in Mesnières-en-Bray. It's the work of two talented sculptors from Pays de Bray, Jacques and Juliette Damville, who have created a remarkable collective artwork here.

On entering the *nef végétale*, as the artists named the sculpture with its plant motifs, you get the impression that the fish becomes a vessel and yourself a passenger aboard a strange Noah's Ark.

A multitude of animals engraved or stamped, created by students from the Pays de Bray colleges involved in the project, decorate the terracotta tiles that make up the interior walls.

Speech balloons composed by students in a writing workshop decorate the engraved tiles, reproducing long strips of unfurled paper, inviting visitors on a journey through words. The fish's two eyes, covered in mosaic tiles, call to mind Captain Nemo's *Nautilus*.

Outside, the richness of the decoration comes to life: figureheads, countless sphinxes, fauna welcoming travellers, and a mast with a crow's nest designed to host migratory birds. Their harmony and elegance reflect the presence, just a few steps away, of Mesnières castle, a true source of inspiration for this multicultural collaboration between artists and students, within the framework of a European project supported by the local association Chemins de Traverse.

This artwork embodies the spirit of the great Renaissance faience artists: Masseo Abaquesne in Rouen and Bernard Palissy in Paris.

The plan over time is for the vessel to be covered in greenery. Mother Nature is expected to dress the uppers and sides with a green mane and take over the numerous specially designed sandstone pockets.

VAL-YGOT V1 LAUNCH SITE, ARDOUVAL

Ancestor of long-range missile

Site open to public on D99 between Bellencombre and Pommeréval
Guided tours: Association de Sauvegarde du Site du V1 du Val-Ygot, Ardouval:
02 35 83 90 66 or 02 35 93 15 04 – henry.bocquet@wanadoo.fr
Information available at Bosc-Eawy tourist office:
02 35 83 21 24 – cc.bosc.eawy@wanadoo.fr

At the edge of Eawy forest, in the commune of Ardouval, a site unique in France is open to visitors: the launch base of the V1 missiles built by the Germans in 1943. The ramp, aimed at London, is accompanied by all the buildings required for this function.

This site, enhanced by the Office National des Forêts and run by a local association, showcases the tracks and other operational facilities of a V1 launch base (see below) under cover of the forest.

The site features a storage shelter for V1 missiles and the fuel stocks, an assembly workshop for the V1s, handling tracks for the V1s, officers' quarters, and the highlight of the visit: the non-magnetic (meaning it contains no ferrous metal) 'cathedral' designed to calibrate the missile's magnetic compass to maintain its course towards London. Additionally there is a 42-metre launch ramp with a restored V1 in the starting position. The entire complex was built using reinforced concrete, following the techniques experimented with on the Atlantic Wall.

From Dunkirk to Cherbourg, 400 ramps (including 120 in Seine-Maritime) were installed by Hitler to bombard London and English ports, in an attempt to prevent a British landing in continental Europe.

The Val-Ygot site, completed by Christmas 1943, never became operational as it was immediately bombed by the Allies thanks to information provided by the local Resistance.

Nevertheless, over 3,000 V1s struck London between 13 June and 31 August 1944, resulting in 6,000 deaths and over 18,000 injury victims. But the technology was not entirely reliable, and an estimated quarter of the V1s launched fell on nearby villages, also causing death and injury.

Normandy is riddled with V1 launch bases, but the Val-Ygot site is the only one to have been reconstructed.

In the Caumont caves (Eure department), near La Bouille, is a German underground factory to produce fuel for V2 rockets, which can only be visited during Journées de la Spéléo (Caving Days, last Sunday of September).

In contrast, in the Pas-de-Calais, La Coupole site has been reconstructed and is open to the public.

As the ancestor of long-range missiles, the V1 was the first unmanned flying torpedo. It could travel 250 km in 25 minutes.

WOODCUTTER'S HUT
IN EAWY FOREST

Remains of a 'carcahoux'

Between Saint-Saëns and Pomméreval via D12
Turn right towards Église des Ventes-Saint-Rémy (76680), then continue to plot 360 of Eawy forest and follow signs
Open access

At the start of a two-hour discovery trail in Eawy, one of the most beautiful beech forests in France, you'll find a 'carcahoux' or lumberjack's shelter, also known as *la loge au père Achille*. It's named Achille after the man who built it, with the help of the Association des Amis de la Forêt d'Eawy and the Office National des Forêts.

Such huts were built by the lumberjacks themselves for shelter at the logging site where they were working. They'd trace a 3-metre-diameter circle on the ground, gather 5-metre poles, cross them at the top, secure them with hazel sticks, and line the sides with freshly picked ferns. An entrance small enough to retain heat from the central fireplace, a few wooden beds also filled with ferns, and simple furniture made from branches allowed a team of two or three men to live on-site from November to April in the logging season.

Similar huts can also be found in the Eu and Lyons forests. It's believed that they were brought by seasonal workers from Auvergne who came to Normandy's forests for logging, charcoal production, or ripsawing railroad sleepers.

Following the *sentier des écoliers* (schoolchildren's trail), you'll discover along the way over 30 tree species to identify with the help of information boards. Some have remarkable shapes, such as the beech tree with four trunks and five heads that heralds the hut. Continue along the trail and you'll reach Camp Souverain, a large clearing where Louis XIV is said to have entertained a charming lunch companion. Deviating slightly from the circuit, a few hundred metres away you'll find an underground cavity called the *puits merveilleux* (marvellous well). This man-made sinkhole, possibly used for storage, was dug into the ground and can be accessed through a tiny opening that widens like a giant bottle. Legend has it that a carriage and horses were swallowed up in there.

NEARBY

Another educational trail In Pays de Bray was once used by children from the hamlet of Forêt on the way to school in Ferrières-en-Bray. It passes near Manais farm, the original production site of Charles Gervais' *petits suisses* (creamy white cheeses), which was replaced around 1850 by the 7 Gervais dairy, now Danone, in Ferrières-en-Bray.

FERME DE BRAY

Preserving the memory of past artisans

76440 Sommery
02 35 90 57 27 – ferme.de.bray.free.fr
Weekends and public holidays, Easter to All Saints' Day 2pm–6pm
Every afternoon 2pm–6pm July and Aug
Group visits throughout the year on reservation
Guest rooms available on estate
Accessible via Route de Paris at Dieppe D915 (Paris, Gisors, Gournay-en-Bray, Forges-les-Eaux) or via A28 exit Les Grandes Ventes

On the road from Paris to Dieppe, leaving Forges-les-Eaux and its famous casino behind, turn left at the top of a small hill, and Bray Farm estate emerges from the past in its green setting. The farm is a unique and well-preserved example of a rural domain from the 17th century. Among the various restored buildings around the farm, you'll find a grain mill, bread oven, dovecote, chicken coop, and an area devoted to cider-making (granary, press, cellar).

Each building showcases various collections of traditional tools used in the production of cider, flour, or Neufchâtel cheese. Ancient documents and period photographs are also displayed, bringing these objects to life in everyday use. The farm surprises visitors with its realistic presentation and its rich and well-maintained heritage. The mill, bread oven, and press are all in working order.

This all began in 1270 when Raoul de Bray owned a feudal estate known as Hamel, which included a mill and a small dwelling. In 1452, miller Raulin Potier acquired the property. He then obtained the rights to operate the mill and produce flour. This turned out to be a wise decision. Over the centuries, his descendants were able to repurchase the feudal rights as well as the lord's manor. They too became landowners, renting out their lands and mill. Sixteen generations later, visitors are welcomed by Patrice Perrier, along with his grandchildren as worthy representatives of the eighteenth generation. Perrier owns the land (70 hectares), farmhouse (1.5 hectares) and pond (1 hectare), now used for fishing.

ORIENTATION TABLE
AT LA FERTÉ-SAINT-SAMSON

A disorienting orientation table

76440 La Ferté-Saint-Samson
*From Forges-les-Eaux take the D921, drive up to La Ferté-Saint-Samson, park
at church and climb hill to reach orientation table
Open 24/7*

A few kilometres from Forges-les-Eaux, a natural hill turned into a feudal mound offers a vast panorama of part of Pays de Bray. An orientation table designed by Jacques and Juliette Damville, two local sculptors (see p. 256), offers help to visitors wanting to understand the landscape they're admiring. It sheds light on the alchemy and astrology of the Middle Ages.

Made from glazed and water-coloured sandstone, the orientation table presents a 300-degree view of the landscape. The two artists aimed to evoke traditional planets, zodiac signs, and the quest of medieval alchemists who sought to transmute base metals into gold. The seven spheres on the upper table represent the planets revolving around a hollow dome with a representation of the 14th-century sky, surrounded by the signs of the zodiac.

The hill where the orientation table is located, at an altitude of 189 metres, was probably in use before the 10th century. At that time a wooden fortification known as a ferté was built there. After 911, Rollo, a Viking who became the first ruler of Normandy, entrusted Pays de Bray to one of his companions named Eude, whose grandson Gauthier became first lord of La Ferté. It was Gauthier who built the church in 989 and commissioned the feudal mound.

Following the conquest of England in 1066 by William the Conqueror, conflicts between France and England grew. In 1151, Henry II Plantagenet, King of England and Duke of Normandy, attacked La Ferté and razed it to the ground. In 1204, during the annexation of Normandy to France by Philip II (Philip Augustus), La Ferté became part of the royal fortification line. It remained under French control until the Hundred Years' War, when it fell into English hands.

Until the French Revolution, the town of La Ferté was a place of high justice with jurisdiction over about 50 parishes.

Prisoners were tried and executed, exposed on the gallows on the hill called Mont aux Fourches above the former commune of Saint-Samson.

NEARBY

The centre of the former commune of La Ferté, now merged with Saint-Samson, perched on a hill, is frozen in time and well worth a visit. An imposing half-timbered house, known as Maison Henri IV, overlooks another remarkable panorama towards Forges-les-Eaux (private access). The abbey church of Saint-Martin at Sigy-en-Bray, 5 km away, is the only remaining sign of the abbey built in the 11th century by Hugues de la Ferté. In this peaceful village its size and the grandeur of its 13th-century choir are surprising.

WAR MEMORIAL
AT CUY-SAINT-FIACRE

The only war memorial sculpture by François Pompon

Église Saint Martin and Cimetière de Cuy-Saint-Fiacre
4 km from Gournay-en-Bray
François Pompon's cottage: viewable from outside only, closed to the public
For more information: Consult the publications of the Association Les Amis de
l'Ours de Cuy-Saint-Fiacre

I n the late 19th and first third of the 20th centuries, the village of Cuy-Saint-Fiacre was notorious for attracting artists.

In 1921, François Pompon (1855–1933), a wildlife sculptor well-known for his simplified forms and even surfaces, was commissioned to create the war memorial for the commune in 1921, following a subscription appeal launched in 1919. This saved him from hardship as the year 1921 was very difficult for him, having lost his wife Berthe in June. Pompon, who was foreman at Rodin's workshop in the late 19th century and also collaborated with Camille Claudel, was a local resident.

Pompon designed this monument, which stands over 2 metres high, as if the background follows the path of the Sun, starting with the gentle and soothing sunrise in the east. The frontispiece, on the other hand, evokes the harsh reality of death: a cross inscribed with the names of children from the commune who died for France, with a helmet on top. The monument culminates in shadow, facing the setting sun in the west.

The sculptor crowned the monument with a rooster, his wings outspread to symbolise the renewal of hope.

This memorial to those killed in the Great War, offering an allegory of light and darkness, is the only one by this renowned sculptor. Despite his offer, he was not commissioned for the war memorial in Saulieu, his hometown.

The cottage where Pompon lived with his wife Berthe from 1907 to 1921, and then alone until his death in 1933, stands near the church.

Artists in Cuy-Saint-Fiacre

Eugène Baugnies (1842–91), an orientalist known for his painting *La fuite en Égypte* (Flight into Egypt), which is still exhibited in the church, was the first husband of Marguerite de Saint-Marceaux (1850–1930). Marguerite hosted a music salon on Boulevard Malesherbes in Paris and in Cuy-Saint-Fiacre. The salon was open to musicians, artists and emerging writers. Prominent figures such as Debussy, Ravel, Fauré, Colette, and Marcel Proust were frequent visitors. One of the Baugnies' three sons, Jacques, created a rare large-scale painting inspired by the Nabi decorative arts style, which is mounted on one of the walls of the church. Marguerite's second husband, René de Saint-Marceaux (1845–1915), was a sculptor. He gifted the church with a stone statue of the Virgin and Child of great purity. He also prepared his future tomb in the cemetery, where he depicted himself lying down with a sculptor's chisel, alongside Marguerite holding a sheet of music. He died in 1915 without being able to complete his tomb, which François Pompon finished in a much understated style.

ABBÉ PIERRE'S OFFICE BEDROOM

'Ici, j'ai fait mon nid'

Centre Abbé Pierre-Emmaüs, Esteville
280 Route de Cailly – 76690 Esteville
02 35 23 87 76 – centre-abbe-pierre-emmaus.org
Daily 10am–6pm
Closed 24 Dec–3 Jan (inclusive)

The Abbé Pierre-Emmaüs Centre in Esteville, where the celebrated priest lived from 1991 to 1998, lets visitors explore his preserved office bedroom as well as the chapel where he officiated. The inscription on his worktable reads: *Avec vous, le véritale hommage c'est de continuer* (With you, the true homage is to carry on). Cluttered with reclaimed wooden shelves, humorously referred to as the 'Louis Caisse style' (a play on words referencing the royal opulence of Louis XVI), the office looks as if it has just been vacated.

Since 2012 there's been a memorial site dedicated to Abbé Pierre open to visitors, consisting of 10 exhibition rooms and a permanent display in the stopover point within the wooded park. The memorial retraces his journey in France and around the world.

The exhibition design is simple and unadorned, reflecting his character. It was achieved with limited resources and a spirit of solidarity, yet is rich in documents and oral testimonies. The depth and relevance of his commitment and legacy are highlighted, the major injustices of our time across the world denounced.

'He tried to love'

As the founder of the Communauté des Chiffonniers d'Emmaüs (Emmaüs Community of Ragpickers), Abbé Pierre (real name Henri Groués) gained recognition during the harsh winter of 1954, prior to which he'd been a resistance fighter during the war and a member of parliament in 1945. During a broadcast on Radio Luxembourg (the precursor to RTL), he made a memorable appeal for the right to housing for the homeless, sparking a real 'uprising of kindness.' From then on he worked tirelessly towards housing the poor in France and around the world. He also supported Coluche in setting up the Restos du Cœur (Restaurants of the Heart). Abbé Pierre, recognised as the favourite personality of the French for several consecutive years, died on 22 January 2007. *Il a essayé d'aimer* (He tried to love) is the epitaph on his very simple tomb in the village cemetery, 600 metres from his bedroom. Following an official ceremony at Notre-Dame de Paris, celebrated by the Archbishop of Paris in the presence of the President of the Republic, Abbé Pierre was laid to rest on a snowy day in the intimacy of Esteville's Emmaüs companions'

section. His body rests beneath a cast-iron Christ, surrounded by his early companions: Lucie Goutaz, his faithful secretary, social worker and co-founder of the movement, along with other companions from the early days, such as Charles Gilardeau, Lucie Gouët, Pierre Drouault and René Combon, among others. Each day, admirers from around the world flock to pay their final respects to someone who was a role model for them.

The Esteville Emmaüs stopover point continues to welcome companions who want to have a rest.

From 1983 to 1991, Abbé Pierre also found solace as a guest of the monks at Abbaye de Saint-Wandrille near Caudebec-en-Caux (Seine-Maritime), where he would quietly pray and seek spiritual solace.

MONUMENTAL CARILLON AT NOTRE-DAME-DE-BONDEVILLE

Unique in Europe

Place Victor Schoelcher, 97 Route de Dieppe, facing town hall
76960 Notre-Dame-de-Bondeville
02 32 82 35 00
Chimes every hour and at noon every day

In the heart of the town of Notre-Dame-de-Bondeville, many passers-by are surprised by an astounding monumental sculpture. '*Ars Sonora*, abbey and industry' is how Jean-Marc Bonnard, designer of this contemporary carillon, describes his work, which draws inspiration from the religious and industrial heritage of the commune.

The religious aspect is represented by Gothic arches like those of a Cistercian convent that existed from the 12th to the 17th centuries, and also by a a Merovingian church discovered by chance near the town hall as the foundations were being laid for the Mathilde de Rouvres media library in 1999.

The industrial heritage of the commune is suggested by its chimneys, incorporated into the sculpture as steel columns. Notre-Dame-de-Bondeville was the first commune in France to open a legal *indiennes** factory in 1762, and is also home to the first industrial museum in France: the Vallois ropeworks (see following double-page spread).

Bonnard, an eclectic artist with many interests as visual artist, designer and sculptor, is also a professor at the École des Beaux-Arts in Saint-Étienne. To create this musical sculpture he collaborated with the Paccard company, manufacturers of bells in Annecy since 1800.

This is therefore the first musical sculpture in France with a carillon – unique in Europe. This carillon, consisting of 48 tuned bells, was installed at the end of 2009. It marks the hours with pre-recorded melodies ranging from folk songs to jazz, classical music and popular songs, but for special events such as weddings or concerts it can also be played using a piano keyboard. With a range of four octaves and six levels of hammer strikes, the instrument can be played from pianissimo to fortissimo.

For a few years the monument took over from the carillon of Rouen cathedral, which was built in 1920 and currently has 56 bells. The Rouen carillon was out of service for a long time but resumed operation after its bells were recast in 2015 and 16 bells were added. The cathedral now has the second largest carillon in France in terms of the number of bells, after the one in Chambéry.

---

* *Painted or printed fabrics manufactured in Europe between the 17th and 19th centuries.*

WATERWHEEL AT MUSÉE INDUSTRIEL DE LA CORDERIE VALLOIS

An industrial museum in a stunning green setting

76960 Notre-Dame-de-Bondeville
02 35 74 35 35
On the former N27 Rouen-Dieppe road, 800 metres after Notre-Dame-de-Bondeville town hall on the way from Rouen, next to intercommunal swimming pool
Daily 1.30pm–6pm, except 1 Jan, 1 May, 1 Nov, 11 Nov, 25 Dec
Machines in operation at 2pm, 3pm, 4pm, 5pm
Guided tour

The industrial museum of La Corderie Vallois is one of the few museums in France to showcase the functioning of textile machines from the late 19th century.

The current factory was built in 1821 as a spinning mill on the site of a paper mill, along the Cailly river. At a time when electricity was not yet invented, factories were built on multiple levels, with plenty of windows to capture maximum light and so work from dawn to dusk.

The spinning mill continued to operate, albeit with difficulties, until 1862 when the American Civil War disrupted the cotton supply. An attempt was made to convert to linen spinning but the mill was eventually sold to Jules Vallois, who transferred his ropemaking business from Saint-Martin-du-Vivier.

Using his pre-1860 braiding machines carried by mules between Saint-Martin-du-Vivier and Notre-Dame-de-Bondeville, from 1885 onwards Vallois also acquired Scottish and English machines to cable and braid cotton.

He developed a business supplying the Normandy spinning mills, as they needed vast quantities of cords and ropes to operate the industrial spindles that replicated the work of a spinning wheel.

By 1978, when the company closed down, there were only three employees left, together with the equipment. A significant part of this dated back to the late 19th century.

Conversion into a museum took 16 years. Seine-Maritime conseil général, which already manages a network of departmental museums, agreed to oversee this 'new' museum. The factory was studied and archaeologically restored, ensuring that the machines could continue to work while welcoming visitors.

The result lives up to expectations, with the waterwheel driven by the Cailly river still moving all the preserved machines. You'll find yourself transported into the ambiance of 19th and early 20th-century textile factories.

BREAD OVEN
OF LA PANNEVERT

Buy your bread baked in an 18th-century oven

Expotec 103 Centre d'Histoire Sociale
13 Rue Saint-Gilles
76000 Rouen
expotec103.fr
Bread baking and sales: 1st and 3rd Fri of months March–Nov

Rouen's Centre for Social History (CHS) has been uncovering the forgotten heritage of the city since the 1980s. The association is responsible for the *route des moulins* (mill trail), a picturesque pedestrian circuit along the Robec river (a tributary of the Seine that brought prosperity to the city). In 1989 an 18th-century bread oven was installed within this circuit, just a stone's throw from the city centre yet unknown to many locals. Waterwheels had been used along this watercourse since the Middle Ages. Some were dedicated to the milling industry, while others crushed plants for dyes or compressed woollen cloth made in Rouen to tighten the weave.

Twice a month in Rouen, anyone interested can watch bread baking in a communal oven known as a four banal (traditional oven). Before the Revolution, the common people had to use the overlord's facilities to bake their bread, in exchange for paying a tax called 'le ban', which gave the oven its name.

The bread oven stands alongside the Pannevert wheat mill and the market gardeners' house. This well-knit group, named Site de la Pannevert, has contributed to revitalising a peripheral area as a green lung of the city.

The communal oven comes from a former agricultural holding in Croisy-sur-Andelle, about 20 km from Rouen. It was saved in the nick of time by the association before it could be used as firewood. The timber-framed construction with its flint and tiles roof was completely dismantled and reassembled in three months in 1989, thanks to the efforts of about a dozen people participating in heritage restoration projects led by the CHS in partnership with the job centre. This project marked the beginning of a 10-year collaboration between the two bodies, resulting in the restoration or rehabilitation of 150 heritage sites in Normandy, such as Ry farm, the mills of Veules-les-Roses, and the Clarenson textile factory at Elbeuf.

The oven, severely damaged in an arson attack in 2013, was restored to its original state through fundraising efforts. It's still in working order and serves its purpose thanks to two enthusiastic retired bakers. They sell their products for a token price twice a month – brioches, apple turnovers and loaves of bread, all cooked in a wood-fired oven.

MASONIC SYMBOLISM OF TOMB OF CARDINALS OF AMBOISE

A Freemason architect in Rouen cathedral

Cathédrale Notre-Dame
76000 Rouen
Daily except Monday mornings
Guided tour of the baptistery, Chapelle de la Vierge, and crypt (normally closed to the public): daily during school holidays and weekends throughout the year, 2.30pm

In Rouen cathedral's chapel of the Virgin stands the monumental mausoleum of the cardinals of Amboise, a work commissioned by the famous Cardinal Georges I of Amboise (1460–1510) from the great architect Roland Le Roux. He completed the project between 1516 and 1521 under the direction of the cardinal's grandson and successor, Georges II of Amboise (1488–1550). Both cardinals are buried there. At the top is an altar and a wooden retable carved and gilded by sculptor and painter Jean Racine in 1643.

The two cardinals are shown kneeling, grandson behind grandfather, who extends his hands in supplication to the Virgin. On the canopy are Christ, the Virgin and various apostles, and just below them the patron saints of these two holy figures, including St George piercing the dragon with his lance. Finally, on the base, statues represent the Virtues. While this monumental ensemble illustrates the evolution of Renaissance art in Rouen, behind the appearance of piety lies a decidedly unorthodox Masonic message attributed to Racine, who sought to leave the mark of his initiation into Freemasonry.

On the canopy, Christ is handing the setsquare to the apostle St Andrew, while the virtue of Prudence displays the compass. Setsquare and compass, above and below, have always been Masonic symbols and in this sense their initiatory interpretation goes well beyond the devotional piety reflected by the artist. St Andrew is depicted with a cross in the shape of an X. According to the Gospel According to St John, he was a disciple of John the Baptist but left to follow Jesus Christ. Andrew was considered the intermediary between the Announcer (John the Baptist) and the Announced (Jesus Christ). The name comes from the Greek *Andrós*, which means man, which in turn gives *Alexandrós*, 'defender of men'. Among the Masonic initiates versed in Judeo-Christian Kabbalistic doctrine, St Andrew is seen as the one who will establish the foundations of the New Jerusalem (or Celestial Jerusalem – the spiritual goal of the 29th degree of the Ancient and Accepted Scottish Rite's Grand Scottish Knight of Saint Andrew). That's why he is receiving the square from Christ, as seen here. On each side of this scene are a nobleman and a lady whose poses describe one of the seven secret signs of the 29th Masonic degree, the Sign of Water – the right hand placed on the heart and lowered until it reaches the side of the body.

The apostle St Andrew's presence in Freemasonry dates back to 1593, when James VI of Scotland founded the Royal Order of the Rose-Cross with 32 knights of the Order of Saint Andrew of the Thistle. At that time the king was Grand Master of the Operative Masons of Scotland, but during exile in France of his successor James II the Order of the Scottish Masters of Saint Andrew was founded in 1659, a name that has never been abandoned by the movement.

On the moral plane, the setsquare symbolises impartiality, justice and uprightness. It constitutes the jewel of the Masonic Worshipful Master's function because he must be the most upright and just in the Lodge and carry out his duty with absolute impartiality.

The virtue of Prudence (*Sapientia*), at the base of the retable, holds a Masonic compass instead of the usual book of iconography. The symbolic

action of the compass, with its duality (two branches) and union (their junction), is one of the strongest symbols of Freemasonry, along with the setsquare and sacred scripture. All three are called the great jewels and great lights of Freemasonry. The compass represents measurement and justice. In its right hand, the virtue also holds the mirror of wisdom into which it gazes.

Ancient philosophy grouped all morality into four cardinal virtues or principles, upon which all others depend: Justice, Prudence, Fortitude (or Courage) and Temperance. Freemasonry recognises and encourages the practice of the four cardinal virtues, in addition to the three theological virtues (Faith, Hope and Charity – the highest form of Love), and represents them through acorns suspended at the four corners of a Masonic Lodge.

Unlike the cardinal virtues, acquired through constant habit, the theological virtues aren't acquired through human effort. They are virtues taught in the writings of St Paul, so are called theological (imparted by God). For these virtues, man surpasses himself in order to attain Supreme Perfection.

MAISON
DE L'ANNONCIATION

Symbolism of the 'dry' path of alchemy

Rue Eugène Dutuit, next to presbytery at No. 5
76000 Rouen

Next to the presbytery at No. 5, and not far from the church of Saint-Maclou (also known as Saint-Malo – one of the seven saints of Brittany), stands a strange Gothic house dating from the 15th century. The house is named for the sculptures of the Annunciation of the Blessed Virgin Mary on its entrance pediment, accompanied by numerous motifs from the alchemical Great Work.

Although the builder of this house is unknown, its restoration is recorded after a fire that broke out in 1520. The street, which used to be Rue Malpalu, was renamed Rue Eugène Dutuit in 1886 as a tribute to an antiquarian who financed the reconstruction work after the fire in the church district.

The House of the Annunciation was probably built by a member of a wealthy family closely associated with the Benedictine Order of St Maclou. Renowned alchemists were closely connected with this monastic order, and some Benedictine monks themselves were great alchemists, such as Basil Valentine in the 15th century.

Alchemy is accomplished through two paths, known as the wet and the dry. The wet path involves progressive, slow but reliable metallic experiments conducted in the presence of a couple, as their meeting is like the contact of two chemical substances. The main element of these operations is water. Boiling on a gradually intensifying fire, it evaporates while the raw material appears at the bottom of the alembic. This phase is called the Annunciation.

In the dry path the dominant element is fire. The alchemist works alone and shortens the time to reach the goal, which is very risky.

The dry path is represented by the dry tree with knots – the 'knots' of the soul that the adept will 'untie' as quickly as possible in the pursuit of spiritual enlightenment, while outwardly obtaining alchemical gold.

The wooden facade of the House of the Annunciation recalls the tree with its knotted bark, representing the dry path. And although the scene with the Virgin corresponds to a phase of the wet path, it's also present in the dry path.

It symbolically announces the imminent birth of the Philosophical Stone (Christ), with which the Raw Material (Mary) is impregnated, after the Angel (state of spiritual consciousness) has announced the state of Grace (or the means to safely achieve the goal).

Below the Archangel Gabriel are the carved busts of an angel (representing condensations, the spiritual principle) and a human (representing dissipations, the material principle).

Mary is surmounted by a cherub's head (symbolising the ascent of condensations), and the Archangel by the head of a Sylvanus, a kind of faun (symbolising the descent of dissipations).

In the centre, the fleur-de-lis topped with a dragon coiled upon itself represents the alchemical Annunciation. The hermetic sense is given by the dragon, symbolising secret wisdom.

Below the lily is a coat of arms decorated with ropes, knots and a cross – probably an allegory of the alchemical dry path that this building was supposed to represent.

What is alchemy?

During the Middle Ages and Renaissance, most religious orders considered alchemy (from the Arabic word *al-kimiya* or divine chemistry) as the art of the Holy Spirit or the royal art of the divine creation of the world and humanity. The art was closely connected with Orthodox Roman Catholic doctrine.

Practitioners divide alchemy into two main aspects. The first is spiritual, which exclusively concerns the illumination of the soul, transforming impure elements of the body into refined states of spiritual consciousness, also known as the path of penitents. The other is laboratory alchemy, known as the path of philosophers, which replicates in the laboratory the alchemical universe of transmuting the impure elements of nature into noble metals like silver and gold. These two practices are usually pursued together, becoming a path of the humble, where humility is that of the prostrated facing the grandeur of the universe reproduced in the laboratory (from the Latin *labor* and *oratorium*). The alchemy of the soul (internal) is expressed externally in the laboratory.

Those who practice laboratory alchemy solely in search of silver and gold, neglecting the essential aspects of realisation of the soul, will fail and become charlatans. They may have extensive knowledge but certainly lack the necessary moral qualities. To avoid the fate of charlatan (and it was this kind of heretic that was condemned by the Church), the adept must balance mind and heart, culture and moral qualities, penance and humility, in order to become a true philosopher.

LA TOUR DE LA PUCELLE

The final resting place of Joan of Arc

102 Rue Jeanne d'Arc
76000 Rouen
Admission free

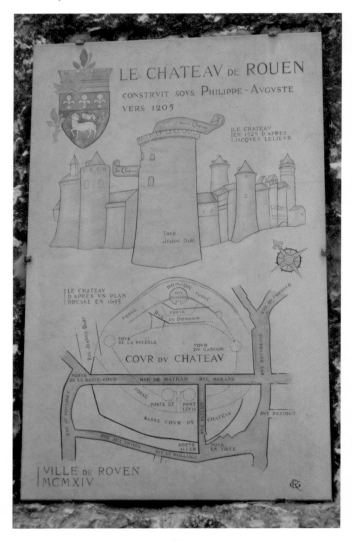

While the history of Joan of Arc is intimately linked to the city of Rouen, it's not generally known that the Maid of Orléans was imprisoned and tried in Rouen at a castle built in 1204 by Philip Augustus (Philip II of France). Only a few remnants survive from this imposing structure. The first is a perfectly preserved keep: Tour Jeanne d'Arc on Rue de Bouvreuil, well known to the people of Rouen, where Joan was held and questioned.

About 50 metres away, at No. 102 Rue Jeanne d'Arc, are the remains of the Tour de La Pucelle (The Maid's Tower), largely unknown to city residents and tourists. Behind an imposing wooden door in a circular paved courtyard, lie the foundations of a keep (as well as a stone staircase and well). Joan was imprisoned here from 25 December 1430 to 30 May 1431, the day of her execution. It's still easy to imagine what this tower was like, although only the foundations remain.

In the early 15th century, The Maid of Orléans led French troops in victorious battles against the English armies, repulsing the siege of Orléans and eventually leading the dauphin Charles to his coronation in Reims, thus changing the course of the Hundred Years' War. Joan, captured by the Burgundians in Compiègne and abandoned by her king, was sold to the English by Jean de Luxembourg. She was ultimately imprisoned in Rouen from December 1430 and tried for heresy. Her trial took place partly in the imposing keep that still stands. There are also writings that attest to Joan being brought to the ground floor of this same tower on Wednesday 9 May 1431, in a fruitless attempt to intimidate her by facing her tormentors and their instruments of torture. Joan's execution, by burning at the stake, took place in public at the Place du Vieux-Marché in Rouen on 30 May 1431. Her ashes were thrown into the Seine.

WOODWORK
AT ABBATIALE SAINT-OUEN

A striking view of Gothic architecture and the city

76000 Rouen
Accessible only on certain dates and Heritage Days
Inquire at Rouen tourist office: 02 32 08 32 40
Reservation required, limited number of places

Access to the higher reaches of churches is rarely possible, and one of the reasons why the roofing often passes unnoticed. However, Normandy possesses some of the most interesting and oldest such woodwork in France.

Saint-Ouen abbey-church is remarkable for the length (137 metres), width (11 metres between the pillars), and height of its vaults (33 metres), above which is the woodwork. You can climb up there via a staircase passing through the Salle des Marmousets, above the portal of the same name, which long housed the abbey archives and is decorated with small figures at the corners.

Next comes the triforium gallery, offering a striking view of the depth of the transept and nave on three levels (grand arcades, triforium, high windows), showcasing the sheer drop and audacious window bays.

Finally you reach the roof, which was rebuilt between 1318 and 1525. This is a characteristic and meticulously crafted example of Gothic carpentry, allowing for very daring architecture and the use of thinner sections of wood.

From there you can also visit the belfry, which supports the bells and prevents their movement from undermining the masonry.

Walking on the outside of the roofs also lets you contemplate the daring architecture of the choir with its flying buttresses, the former abbey garden that has become the City Hall garden on one side and Place du Général de Gaulle on the other.

ATOMIC SHELTER
OF SEINE-MARITIME
CONSEIL GÉNÉRAL

16

A relic of the Cold War

Hôtel du Département
Quai Jean Moulin
76000 Rouen
02 35 03 55 55
The atomic shelter can be viewed for free, on reservation, as part of visit to
Hôtel du Département de Seine-Maritime (allow 2 hours for visit)

I n the late 1990s Seine-Maritime conseil général took over the premises of the former prefecture, which were built between 1957 and 1965. As a result, the department inherited an atomic shelter capable of accommodating up to 250 people, constructed at the height of the Cold War.

The shelter, included in the prefecture's initial construction plans in the 1960s, was never used as such and is now a massive archive storage space.

You can make a reservation to explore this astonishing place, concealed behind several large metal and concrete doors over 70 cm thick. Everything was designed, with the knowledge of the time, to preserve the lives and safety of those with civic responsibilities: the prefect, mayors, gendarmes, police officers, firefighters, doctors and so on.

On the ground floor, long corridors lead to living space before opening onto the command room, where all information would have been centralised in the event of an atomic attack.

Upstairs, numerous small rooms were planned to accommodate survivors as comfortably as possible. Bicycles connected to dynamos are still installed in one corner. This system was supposed to provide electricity and ventilation to the shelter during the confinement period.

Despite all these precautions, this shelter would have been completely ineffective in protecting anyone from radiation – the walls weren't completely sealed. Also it was built underground, below the level of the Seine, and therefore liable to water infiltration.

LA ROUE D'ABANDON DES ENFANTS DE ROUEN

17

Abandon a child safely

Germont entrance of Rouen University Hospital
Rue Germont
76000 Rouen
Admission free

'From these relationships, five children were born, all of whom were sent to the Foundling Hospital, with so little care to recognise them one day that I did not even keep the date of their birth.' This is how Jean-Jacques Rousseau expressed himself in a letter to the Duchess of Luxembourg in 1761.

The practice of abandoning children at birth was common in the past, often through poverty or illegitimacy. To combat infanticide and abortion, the abandonment towers or foundlings' wheels were made mandatory in major French cities, starting in 1811. In Seine-Maritime there were three such: in Rouen, Le Havre and Dieppe. Only the one at the Hospice of Rouen, established in 1813, remains.

The tower consisted of a wooden turnstile embedded in a window in the wall and fitted with a bell. The mother would place the baby inside with some distinctive signs in its swaddling clothes for future identification, ringing the bell before vanishing. A nun would then take charge of the child. Hundreds of children were abandoned each year.

The use of these towers was definitively stopped in Rouen in 1862 and officially in France in 1904, after most of them were replaced in the 19th century by offices for the admission of abandoned children.

For more information on foundlings' wheels, see following double-page spread.

NEARBY
Registers of abandoned children ⑱

Musée Flaubert et d'Histoire de la Médecine
Centre Hospitalier Universitaire de Rouen
51 Rue de Lecat, 76000 Rouen
02 35 15 59 95 – musée.flaubert@wanadoo.fr
Tues 10am–12.30pm and 2pm–6pm, Wed–Sat 2pm–6pm
Groups received mornings on reservation

Abandoned children were registered in a ledger with the date they were found and identifying marks (remarks) accompanying the child. These marks often included a playing card, a piece of the mother's personal fabric, and sometimes a note of explanation. The registers, along with their notes and remarks, are preserved at the Flaubert Museum and History of Medicine in Rouen and in Seine-Maritime Departmental Archives. Reading them gives an insight into 19th-century living conditions.

Foundlings' wheels (roues d'abandon)

As early as 787 a Milan priest named Dateo is said to have placed a shell outside his church to collect abandoned newborns. While the first organised initiatives to care for abandoned children took place at the Hospice des Chanoines in Marseille from 1188 onwards, it was Pope Innocent III (1160–1216, pope from 1198 until his death) who institutionalised this practice. Witnessing the terrible sight of abandoned children's corpses floating through Rome in the Tiber, he decided to implement a procedure to save them. Installed at the gates of convents and designed to preserve the anonymity of parents forced into this situation, the 'wheels of the innocents' consisted of a rotating cradle accessible from the outside. The child was placed in it and a bell rung to alert the nuns inside the convent. They could then rotate the wheel and bring the baby inside. It is worth noting that access to the wheel was protected by a grid calibrated to allow only small newborns to pass through.

This system, out of use since the 19th century, has had to be reintroduced throughout Europe over the past 20 years because of a significant increase in child abandonment. There are 80 such wheels in Germany and several dozen in countries such as Italy or the Czech Republic. Japan has even recently installed one. Historical abandonment towers can be seen in the Vatican, Pisa, and Florence (see the guides *Secret Tuscany*, *Secret Florence* and *Secret Rome*), Bayonne, and Barcelona (*Secret Barcelona*, all published by Jonglez).

In France it was St Vincent de Paul who first had abandonment towers built in 1638. There were around 251 of them in the country. In 1787, Necker estimated the number of foundlings at 40,000 out of a population of 26 million. From 1640 to 1789, the Hôpital des Enfants Trouvés (Foundlings' Hospital) in Paris took in 390,000 children. In 1863, the abandonment towers were theoretically closed and replaced by 'admission offices' where mothers could leave their children while receiving advice. The towers were abolished in 1904 and, in 1941 under the Vichy regime, a decree was issued regarding the protection of births, allowing anonymous childbirth.

Famous foundlings

Among the most celebrated abandonment wheel foundlings are Pope Gregory VII, Genghis Khan and Jean-Jacques Rousseau.

ANGÉLIQUE DU COUDRAY'S 'GHOST'

A spectacular birthing dummy for training midwives

Musée Flaubert et d'Histoire de la Médicine
Centre Hospitalier Universitaire de Rouen
51 Rue de Lecat
Rouen 76000
02 35 15 59 95
Tues 10am–12.30pm and 2pm–6pm
Wed–Sat 2pm–6pm

The centrepiece of the Flaubert Museum and History of Medicine, the birthing dummy from the collections of the Hôtel-Dieu, Rouen's former hospital, is also known as the fantôme (ghost) due to its realistic appearance.

This tool with a pedagogical purpose was devised in the 18th century by midwife Angélique du Coudray. She obtained a royal patent that allowed her to travel around France for 23 years from 1759, sharing her knowledge with numerous young women and training them in the skills of midwifery.

To address the ignorance of midwives, which led to a high mortality rate for both infants and mothers, she provided lessons to carefully

selected young girls with 'educational capacity.' During the six- to eight-week training programme, apprentice midwives would handle these models on a daily basis. As most of the students were illiterate, lessons were sometimes translated into local dialects and demonstrations played a crucial role in learning. Du Coudray is estimated to have trained around 5,000 midwives using her birthing tool.

The dummy was designed to be as realistic as possible, with scrupulous attention to detail of the female anatomy, both internal and external. It was made from an actual pelvic bone, as confirmed by a radiograph conducted in 2004 at the University Hospital Centre of Rouen. The bone is believed to have been exhumed from a mass grave, forming the basis onto which a complex structure was built – a combination of metal, leather and fabric. The fully retractable dummy consists of many additional parts to simulate the different stages of childbirth and address complications associated with delivery, such as a full-term foetus, the head of a stillborn foetus, a full-term uterus (with ribbons to indicate cervical dilation) and a scale representation of the female genitalia.

The reason for the exceptional condition of the dummy at the Flaubert Museum is thought to be that this particular specimen was never used for demonstrations, just as a model for restoring the 15 other dummies at the Hôtel-Dieu, now gone missing.

This dummy, however, remains a valuable testament to a significant contribution to the advancement of obstetric science.

PACIFIC VAPEUR CLUB LOCOMOTIVE

A locomotive named Princesse

BP 115
76300 Sotteville-lès-Rouen
02 35 72 30 55
pacificvapeur.free.fr – pacific-vapeurclub@orange.fr

Pacific locomotives, prestigious high-speed machines, provided traction for express trains from the 1920s to the 1960s. The 231 G 558 is one of the few still in working order. It was built in 1922 at Nantes by the Batignolles-Chatillon company as part of a series of 283 units. Assigned to different depots, it operated high-speed services on various routes including Paris-Bordeaux via Chartres, Niort and Saintes, Paris-Cherbourg, Paris-Le Havre, and finally Nantes-Le Croisic, where it pulled its last train on 29 September 1968, before being stored at Angers.

The locomotive, revitalised in 1969, was transported to Dieppe for use as a stationary boiler for heating heavy fuel on car ferries for a few months. The French National Railway Company (SNCF) unsuccessfully tried to sell it. On the initiative of a depot traction manager in Sotteville-lès-Rouen, the engine was returned in 1972 after lengthy negotiations. It was transferred for a symbolic 1 franc to the Amicale des Chefs de Traction du Réseau de l'Ouest de la SNCF in 1977.

To showcase the pride of Sotteville-lès-Rouen and the town's railway history, the Pacific Vapeur Club association was founded in January 1983. Its objective was to restore the Pacific 231 G 558 steam engine to working condition, thanks to the relentless dedication of former railway workers. On 8 June 1983 it was classified as 'movable property' among Historic Monuments, along with its tender 22 C 367. Restoration began in 1984 and required 8,000 hours of work. The locomotive was certified by Apave Normandie in November 1985 and approved by the SNCF a few months later. Its inaugural train journey took place from Sotteville-lès-Rouen to Paris-Saint-Lazare on Sunday 29 June 1986.

The Pacific Vapeur Club has also acquired, among other relics, a state luggage van built in 1930, a converted 'Mobile Post Office' wagon (1929) used as an exhibition car, five second-class cars, and a first-class car (Ocem type) from the 1930s.

Retro trains for everyone

The Pacific Vapeur Club association, with a train capacity of 448 seats, organises its own trips departing from Sotteville-lès-Rouen and other stations, following the 'One-day retro train' formula.

On request special trains can also be run for associations, businesses, employee committees, local authorities, etc. These trains are always admired and popular with the public.

TROGLODYTE CHAPELLE DE SAINT-ADRIEN

To marry, stick a pin in St Bonaventure's foot

76240 Belbeuf
Contact: Association des Amis de la Chapelle de Saint-Adrien, 76240 Belbeuf
02 35 80 03 77
chapelle.saintadrien@free.fr
RD-6015, 7 km from Rouen direction Vernon; path crossing private property leads to chapel
Tues 10am–midday and 2pm–5.30pm (5pm Nov–Feb), except school holidays and every other weekend 10am–midday and 2pm–6.30pm (5pm Nov–Feb)

The semi-troglodyte chapel of St Adrian, a former hermitage carved into the limestone cliff that was converted into a priory in the 16th century, was rebuilt in the early 17th century. Used as a wine warehouse during the Revolution, it reverted to worship during the Empire. Restored from 1980 onwards by the Association of Friends of the Chapel with the help of artists from Rouen, the chapel is now open to the public.

In the Middle Ages the original chapel, dedicated to St Roch, was a popular pilgrimage site during the plague. The current chapel houses the statues of the three main saints traditionally invoked against the plague: St Roch, St Sebastian and St Adrian, although Seine boatmen also pray to Adrian along with St Clement.

Legend has it that the two founding hermits, Onumphe and Pancrace, prayed to St Bonaventure by sticking a pin in their flesh to help a young girl find a husband. The news spread, and in imitation of the hermits, people started coming from far and wide to stick a pin in the statue of the saint. The practice was certainly encouraged by the guinguettes (open-air cafés) and hotels that sprang up in the village from 1920 onwards, as well as by the nearby river where people could enjoy themselves on the islands.

The cult became so widespread that the statue of St Bonaventure had to be placed under a glass bell jar: thousands of pins stuck in his foot threatened to destabilise it. But the practice is carried on by attaching pins and ribbons to a cushion placed under the statue.

NEARBY
Le Moulin Rose

At the foot of St Adrian's chapel, *Le Moulin Rose* is a *guinguette* opened in 1927 that has managed to diversify its traditional regulars of pasodoble, waltz and tango dancers to attract a younger audience. It's thought to be one of the oldest dance halls in France.

Also worth exploring is St Adrian's limestone slope overhanging the chapel, home to the highly sought-after *violette de Rouen*, a rare and protected wild pansy.

CULT OF ST EXPEDITUS

23

The patron saint of urgent causes

Église de Freneuse
76410 Freneuse
9am–6pm
Admission free

Many worshippers come to the hillside church of Freneuse to pray to St Expeditus. Although this saint is of long standing, his association with urgent causes does not seem to date back further than the 19th century. He's most often depicted as a Roman legionnaire, holding in his right hand a cross inscribed with the Latin word *hodie* (today), while crushing a crow underfoot with the Latin cras (tomorrow).

Such popular success is undoubtedly due largely to his name, Expédit, which in French sounds like *expéditif* (expedient). In Freneuse his cult can be traced back to 1934 and a marble ex-voto plaque bearing that date, which seems to have replaced a cult dedicated to St Vincent and documented in 1879. There are two ways of expressing vows – depositing ribbons or sometimes strips of paper marked with the vow, or recording it in a notebook. Over 300 ribbons, forming a colourful cascade, partially cover the gate of St Expeditus' chapel.

The notebooks, carefully preserved by the clergy, are available to worshippers. Analysis of the notebooks carried out over three years by

researcher Lionel Dumarche shows that the vast majority of appeals to the saint come from women who make vows for themselves or for others. Contrary to expectations, the vows expressed are less often related to health than to material problems (school and university exams, driver's licences ...) or family and emotional issues (relationships, child custody ...).

Reading these registers, which are accessible to all, is striking for the great moral and physical distress of those who come to pray to St Expeditus, begging him to intercede effectively and rapidly.

St Expeditus is also highly revered in the French department of Réunion in the Indian Ocean, as well as in Lisieux (Calvados) and Houppeville (Seine-Maritime).

In Freneuse church, St Rita is also venerated for healing incurable diseases.

Recommended reading: *Un exemple de dévotion populaire contemporaine, le culte de saint Expédit à Freneuse* (Lionel Dumarche) in *Les saints guérisseurs en Seine-Maritime*, exhibition catalogue, Musée des Traditions et Arts Normands–Château de Martainville, Fécamp, 2006.

A saint by mistake?

We know very little about St Expeditus – even whether he really existed. Certainly he's the origin of a cult as fervent as it is popular, spread worldwide, and already attested in the 16th century, at least in France. Several legends have arisen around this saint, including a claim that the name 'Expeditus' derived from the inscription *spedito* (expedited) found on a package sent to Rome containing the relics of an unknown saint.

The name 'Expeditus' certainly favoured wordplay, as he became the saint of swiftness *par excellence*. Originally invoked for urgent causes, he later became the patron saint of merchants (for the expeditious conduct of business affairs) and navigators. For this reason exam candidates also pray to him so that the deliberations of the examination boards are favourable to them. In Milan, another statue of St Expeditus is preserved in San Nicolao church.

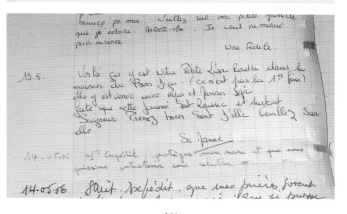

NAPOLEON COLUMN

24

'I wish for my ashes to rest on the banks of the Seine ...'

Napoleon's Testament
76380 Val-de-la-Haye
South-west of Rouen via D51 on right bank of the Seine, and from La Bouille by ferry and then D67 to Sahurs, and finally D51
The column stands at entrance to Val-de-la-Haye village, on the right coming from La Bouille

Along the Seine, on the edge of the former towpath in Val-de-la-Haye, stands a curious column topped with a folded-winged eagle. A quick look around the monument convinces us that it is a commemorative structure linked to Napoleon. The fact is that this column celebrates the return of the emperor's ashes from the island of Saint Helena in 1840, during the July Monarchy, and more specifically marks the transfer of Napoleon's coffin onto another boat.

The *Normandie*, a steam-powered paddleboat, had loaded the 1,200-kg sarcophagus in Cherbourg, where it had arrived on the Belle Poule commanded by Prince de Joinville, a son of King Louis-Philippe. This sailing ship with its considerable draught would have difficulty navigating the Seine.

Furthermore, Louis-Philippe wanted the operation to be discreet so as not to stir up Bonapartist sentiments among the French.

But the *Normandie* couldn't navigate all the way to Paris either, as its funnels wouldn't pass under the bridges beyond Rouen. So another transfer took place on 9 December 1840, downstream from Rouen in Val-de-la-Haye, where the coffin was loaded onto the *Dorade III*, a boat that provided passenger transport between Paris and Rouen. Under close escort, it reached Courbevoie on 14 December and the body was transferred to Les Invalides, Paris, on 15 December by carriage.

The column was erected four years later, in 1844, funded by public subscription.

The emperor's hair

It's worth noting that a box was placed beneath the first stone containing strands of Napoleon's hair, a piece of mahogany from the coffin, and a fragment of the willow that shaded his tomb.

The Musée Roybet Fould at Courbevoie (see *Grand Paris insolite et secret*, also published by Jonglez) preserves another relic related to the transfer of the ashes – wood shavings from Napoleon's coffin.

There's another lock of Napoleon's hair in Copacabana Fort Museum at Rio de Janeiro, Brazil (see *Secret Rio*, also published by Jonglez).

LE QUI VIVE MONUMENT

One of the few monuments commemorating the 1870 war

76530 Moulineaux
Between Grand-Couronne and La Bouille
Leave commune via D3 and take first left (D64), towards Château de Robert le Diable
Le Qui Vive can be seen at intersection below Normandie motorway

One of the most original and rare monuments commemorating the 1870–71 war, given its sad outcome, is undoubtedly *Le Qui Vive* in Moulineaux. Erected in 1901, it overlooks the Seine near Château de Robert le Diable and was designed by sculptor Auguste Foucher. It commemorates the battles that took place on-site, particularly in the castle, from 30 December 1870 to 4 January 1871. It features a 'Mobile' (see below) next to a ruined tower reminiscent of the castle. Sculptor Albert Lambert had added a mascaron depicting Bismarck with bat wings, but that was removed around 1920.

Who were Les Mobiles?

Les Mobiles, or Moblots, referred to soldiers of the Guard Nationale Mobile who served as auxiliaries to the active army in defending the borders of the Empire.

NEARBY

Another monument commemorating the 1870 war: Le Mobile

27310 Saint-Ouen-de-Thouberville
D675 near Maison Brûlée intersection, right at beginning of road towards Pont-Audemer, on the left side; Le Mobile can be seen from the road

This monument, representing an infantryman from the 1870 war, commemorates the heroic fighting of the Mobiles who had to retreat at Maison Brûlée and Saint-Ouen-de-Thouberville. A modest statue had first been erected in the old cemetery in honour of 10 brave Mobiles killed in the battles of 30 and 31 December 1870. The one at Maison Brûlée is more recent and required public subscriptions and contributions. Architect Dupré placed a bronze statue by sculptor Aimé Millet on a hefty stone and brick pedestal, depicting a young man in Mobile uniform with all his equipment. The names were then engraved of the 98 Mobiles and snipers killed in battle there. The 1873 unveiling ceremony in the presence of an estimated crowd of 25,000, some of whom climbed trees to get a better view, foreshadowed the enthusiasm for funerary monuments that would grow after the First World War. In that same year of 1873 two large monuments were erected in the Eure, at Étrepagny and Vernon. Many others would follow, including the statue of the virgin of Graville (see p. 324), the statue in Rouen monumental cemetery, and others at Darnétal, Maromme, etc.

LA CLOSERIE
ENGLISH-STYLE GARDENS

A fragrance of cinema and gardens

76113 Saint-Pierre-de-Manneville
02 35 32 07 06
Take D67 from Saint-Martin-de-Boscherville towards La Bouille and turn left in village
Open access in June or on reservation for other dates

L a Closerie, nestled in the Manneville countryside on a loop of the Seine between Rouen and Duclair, is the sanctuary of writer Anne-Marie Damamme. In June, or on reservation at other times, you can take a friendly tour of the wonderful gardens where literature and art intertwine with plants.

She lives in this peaceful and rather secluded place, surrounded by cats among the flowers, sheltered by dense foliage where old and lesser-known species exude the fragrance of a fantasy world.

Damamme, a subtle storyteller, has written several books, including *Un parfum de tabac blond* (1988), *Le Mah-jong de la neige* (2003), *Des chats comme vous et moi* (2008), and *Escalier par temps de pluie* (2009). As a screenwriter, she also writes for cinema, theatre and television (*Les Capricieux*, *Grand-Hôtel*, *La Mémoire*) and for the stage (*Romanesques*, and an adaptation and translation of Benjamin Britten's libretto *To Make an Opera*).

If she occasionally escapes from La Closerie, it's to wander the streets of London or Paris in search of silverware that will find a place in her home. She generally prefers to travel by train, which holds a romantic allure for her – she is a great admirer of the Orient Express.

Leafing through the souvenir album of La Closerie, you'll inevitably come across Brigitte Bardot. For seven weeks the star filmed most of the scenes for the 1970 cult film *L'Ours et la poupée* (The Bear and the Doll) here under the direction of Michel Deville.

L'Atelier des Champs, a publishing house

In the Damamme family, the daughters are passionate about art. Twins Albane and Donatienne organise an annual exhibition that opens at La Closerie simultaneously with garden visits. This all started when they asked writers to produce a short story inspired by old photos. They then exhibited the collection and produced a compilation. That was their first experience in publishing. Following that, a publishing house was born under the name L'Atelier des Champs. The pace of releases is now accelerating, and collections of short stories and novels are presented at a number of literary festivals, including those in Paris and Caen.

HEURTEAUVILLE PEAT BOG

An exceptional natural site

02 76 51 70 15
Free and open access from dawn to dusk
Via D913, between Bourg Achard and Pont de Brotonne; take D143 towards
Heurteauville, then follow Quai Roger Kervrann (D65) along the Seine

H eurteauville peat bog is one of the 29 sensitive natural sites managed by Seine-Maritime department. It can be explored through three interpretive trails and from various viewpoints.

This wetland, formed 6,000 years ago in the Seine valley, has allowed several metres of peat to build up that harbours a particularly rich fauna and flora.

The peat bog stores rainwater and runoff from the banks of the Seine, acting as a sponge to absorb excess water. In this way the site actively contributes to flood control along the river.

Peat bogs also serve as natural archives of past climates, thanks to the study of pollen or other remains preserved in an oxygen-deprived environment. Towards the end of the 19th century two mummified men with bound wrists were discovered there.

The plant species growing in peat bogs, specific to this environment, are protected because some are endangered. Eleven species of amphibian are present, a sign of the high water quality. As many as 153 bird species have also been recorded.

Industrial use of wetlands: peat for heating, leeches for medicinal purposes ...

As early as 1027, Richard II, Duke of Normandy, confirmed his ancestors' donation of the Harelle pasture to Abbaye de Jumièges. The land, extending over 200 hectares, was a collective property leased to residents of Heurteauville.

The monks allowed local peasants to graze their livestock there. In the mid-18th century there were periodic shortages of wood in Rouen because of the growing population and the proliferation of textile-related industries that burned a lot of firewood, such as dyeing, bleaching and soap-making.

So from 1758 peat from the Heurteauville marsh was used to make briquettes for fuel. From April to November 1827 around a hundred labourers dug out over 2,000 tonnes of peat. With the fall in the price of coal, the extraction of peat for fuel was no longer profitable, and production abruptly stopped in 1831.

Fishing was also carried out in the Harelle, and in 1810 some 30,000 leeches were used for medicinal purposes.

GRAFFITI AT MANOIR DU CATEL

An exceptional and little-known manor

Champ d'Oisel village
76190 Écretteville-lès-Baons
3 km west of Yvetot on RN15, towards Le Havre, take D110 towards
Écretteville-lès-Baons
06 10 21 33 14
Open throughout the year to groups on reservation, and 15 July–30 Aug daily
except Mondays, 10am–1pm and 2pm–5pm
Open for Heritage Days 3rd weekend Sept

Built between 1267 and 1270 on land given to Abbaye de Fécamp by the Duke of Normandy Richard II around the year 1000, Catel manor is one of the oldest and best-preserved fortified houses in Normandy. Still relatively unknown even to locals, it is truly exceptional.

The fortified house, which stands at the centre of an extensive agricultural estate run for the benefit of the abbey, was altered in the 14th, 15th and 16th centuries. Listed as a Historic Monument in 1944 and 1977, the manor has recently been remarkably restored, saving it from ruin.

The upper floor features mullioned windows dating from the 16th century. In the centre of the facade, a fortified stone carriage entrance leads to the courtyard. The entrance was once protected by a drawbridge. Two corner towers balance the facade. There used to be four towers, surrounded by water-filled moats.

Catel manor served as a high court until the Renaissance and was involved in ordinary jurisdiction until the French Revolution. The large (81-hectare) estate, sold as a national asset in 1791, was not broken up.

The manor contains a collection of graffiti, among which three themes stand out: the navy, the church, and death by hanging. Single-masted cutter boats are shown on the walls, sometimes with their crews.

Among the drawings of churches, the one in the nearby commune of Valliquerville can be clearly identified by its characteristic stone spire. Last but not least are the gallows with hanging figures swinging from them inscribed on the walls.

What does 'baon' mean?

The region of '*baons*' is located around Yvetot, with villages such as Écretteville-lès-Baons, Vauville-lès-Baons and Ectot-lès-Baons. The term '*baon*' refers to the assises (benches) of royal jurisdiction, which were held in Baons-le-Comte and known for their severity. The region is said to have adopted that name because of the impact of these proceedings.

ALLOUVILLE-BELLEFOSSE OAK

The most remarkable tree in France?

76190 Allouville-Bellefosse
Access to chapels not allowed

T he Allouville oak, estimated age over 1,200 years, is one of the oldest trees in France and undoubtedly one of the most remarkable.

In 1696 the Abbot of Détroit installed two chapels, one above the other, within the tree trunk that had hollowed out over time. The one on top is Chapelle du Calvaire, which replaced a small hermitage with bed and table. The lower one is Chapelle Notre-Dame de la Paix, decorated with panelling and parquet flooring.

The pious consecration of this prodigious tree almost led to its downfall in 1793, during the French Revolution. Happily it was spared when the village schoolteacher, J.B. Bonheure, had the foresight to write the magical words *Temple de la raison, restauré aux frais du département* (Temple of Reason, restored at departmental expense) on the threatened tree. In 1854 the bishop, Monsignor Blanquart de Bailleul, re-blessed the famous oratory and celebrated Mass there.

In 1981 a burlesque film was even made there by Serge Pénard: *Le Chêne d'Allouville, ils sont fous ces Normands* (The oak of Allouville, they're crazy, these Normans) starring Bernard Menez, Jean Lefebvre, Pierre Tornade, Philippe Nicaud and Alphonse Boudard. The film shows the mayor of Allouville and a local politician campaigning to cut the roots of the millennial oak to widen the road. Opposition comes from the priest and the community who want to save the tree.

Two other remarkable vanished trees

Not far from the oak, in the presbytery gardens, were two other impressive trees, now gone.

Also created by the ingenious abbot, one was a giant hawthorn with a rotunda built around it, complete with floor and windows, which could be entered by climbing a ladder.

It could accommodate up to 12 people for a meal, but the rotunda, known from drawings and testimonies of people who visited in 1780, was destroyed early in the Revolution.

The other was a beech tree shaped like an umbrella that could shelter about 60 people.

A 19th-century industrial town

76164 Rives-en-Seine
From Caudebec-en-Caux, take D81 towards Notre-Dame-de-Gravenchon
In Villequier, park in front of town hall and continue on foot along
departmental road in the same direction
Workers' housing, buildings and walls can be seen on the way

Villequier, a charming residential town on the banks of the Seine with a museum dedicated to Victor Hugo, isn't widely recognised as a prosperous industrial site from 1874 to 1894, thanks to the Établissements Céramiques de Villequier. The town is better known for the tragic drowning of Hugo's daughter Léopoldine Vacquerie and the grave of his wife Adèle in the cemetery. Quarrying alongside the Seine to contain the river led to the discovery of a vast clay deposit. A tuilerie (tilery) was built nearby.

The speciality of this establishment, which employed about a hundred workers, was to hire a sculptor who offered customers not only traditional production but also terracotta artworks (statuettes, medallions, plant pots, ridge tiles, decorative panels ...).

The entire range of products, known from an 1890 commercial catalogue, featured at regional exhibitions in Rouen in 1884 and the 1889 Universal Exhibition in Paris, and some pieces are preserved in local museums.

The factory with its seven chimneys extended over 500 metres. A walk through the town lets you discover buildings and retaining walls made from stacked tiles, ridge tiles, beautiful decorative clay panels under the windows of the former director's house, as well as the workers' housing known as '*LA CITÉ*'.

On the other hand, the few remains of the open-pit and underground extraction are now within private properties and inaccessible.

Production stopped in 1894 when the clay seam was exhausted, and some of the workers were employed at the Argences tilery in Calvados.

ÉGLISE SAINT-JEAN-BAPTISTE AT TRIQUERVILLE

A unique example of metallic religious architecture in Upper Normandy

76476 Port-Jérôme-sur-Seine
D982 between Caudebec and Lillebonne, then at Anquetierville take D28A towards Triquerville
Go up through village to church overlooking Place Saint-Jean-Baptiste
Contact town hall for key: 02 35 38 64 98

The exterior of Triquerville's church of Saint-Jean-Baptiste gives no hint of its precious interior. Built in 1890–91 by engineers Schupp and Pirre from the metallurgical factories in Amiens, this is one of the very few churches in France with a metal structure.

Far from Gothic, Romanesque or Neoclassical styles, the building is punctuated by cast-iron columns, beams and crosspieces, reminiscent of the architecture of the Baltard pavilions (one of which survives at Nogent-sur-Marne in the Parisian region — see *Grand Paris insolite et secret*, also published by Jonglez), popularised by the 1889 Universal Exhibition in Paris.

The building replaced an older church, dating back at least to the 13th century, which was rebuilt in 1530 on a rock and subsequently enlarged several times. This first church, in poor condition, was left to its fate in the second half of the 19th century because of the ongoing dispute between the two dominant families in the commune, the Rives and the Costé, about the means to restore it.

The Marquis of Triquerville, local mayor, who was acquainted with the architect Victor Baltard, acquired a pavilion from the Universal Exhibition and donated the land, providing 91% of the funds required. A bell tower was added to the pavilion, and in less than a year the church was reassembled. It was consecrated on 22 September 1891. The interior has recently been restored.

Église Notre-Dame-du-Travail in Paris, in the 14th arrondissement, is another example of this type of architecture (see *Secret Paris*, also published by Jonglez).

NEARBY

The church overlooks the main square of the village, where the Saint-Jean-Baptiste fountain is located. This used to be an open-air spring where pilgrims came to bathe and walk around the old church thrice in order to be healed. The spring can still be seen at the bottom of a large masonry well topped by a gilded statue of St John the Baptist. This 1980s' arrangement was designed by Jean-Pierre Lefebvre, an architect from Rouen. A bonfire in the saint's honour was also lit on Saint-Jean's day at a nearby crossroads. Behind the church, the Costé de Triquerville family chapel is the site of several tombs of the former lords of Triquerville's descendants. These were transferred to this chapel from the family vault near the castle in the 1960s.

LILLEBONNE MILESTONE

Juliobona, one of the most significant Gallo-Roman settlements in northern France

76170 Lillebonne
02 32 84 02 07
From Rouen via Caudebec-en-Caux (D982) and from Le Havre via A131 then D982
Musée Archéologique de Lillebonne, Place Félix Faure, is now open to the public in a new presentation of the Gallo-Roman settlement

Lillebonne, formerly Juliobona, is chiefly known as home to the most significant Gallo-Roman theatre with an oval stage in northern France (see photo below).

An archaeological museum just opposite the theatre presents the discoveries made during excavations. Among them is an impressive milestone unearthed at Place Carnot in the town centre, preserved in what would have been the forum.

Some analyses suggest that this may not in fact be the forum but rather the edge of a Gallo-Roman portico, and that the milestone may be a Roman column with a dedication to Caesar Carin of Calètes. He was probably an emissary sent to Gaul to fight the Germanic peoples in 282 CE.

From Lillebonne, five Roman roads branched out in all directions: one towards Harfleur (Caracotinum), the port that preceded Le Havre in the Seine estuary; one towards Rouen (Rotomagus) through Caudebec-en-Caux; another towards Lisieux (Lexovium), crossing the Seine at Aizier or Vieux-Port; one towards Étretat, and finally, one to the north that reached Arques, near Dieppe, then Boulogne and the coast. This northern road passed through the ancient Gravinum (now Gréaume, in the commune of Héricourt-en-Caux) after separating from the Lillebonne–Cany road at Fauville-en-Caux.

Milestones

Milestones corresponded to today's kilometre markers and were installed every Roman mile (about 1.5 km). The roads in these regions were rarely paved but had a surface reinforced with gravel, which earned them the names *chaussée de César* (Caesar's road), *chemin perré* (paved road), or *chemin des Romains* (Roman road).

ATELIER-MUSÉE DU TEXTILE AT BOLBEC

The threads of memory

Espace Desgenétais, 5 Rue Auguste Desgenétais – 76210 Bolbec
On road to Lanquetot, 1 km from town hall
Tues, Wed, Thurs, Fri, as well as 1st Sun of month and 3rd Sat of month (except public holidays), 2pm–5pm (guided tour), last departure 3.30pm
For groups, open daily on reservation: 06 38 39 10 17

Bolbec textile workshop-museum, housed in the former Desgenétais spinning mill, is unique in France. It brings together a collection of textile machines that can convert cotton bales directly into finished cotton fabric, covering all the stages of spinning and weaving (carding, voiles, roving, ribbons, yarn, winding, bobbins, warping, sizing,

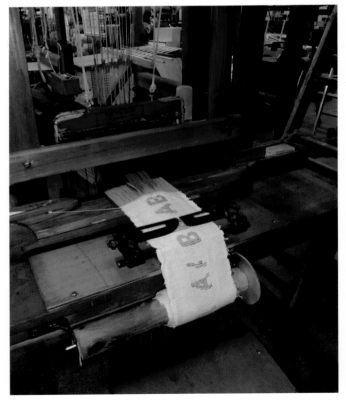

weaving, etc.).

The machines, about 20 in all, are operated in view of the public. They were all salvaged, sometimes as scrap metal, and restored by textile workers and executives belonging to the association Bolbec au Fil de la Mémoire (Bolbec through the Threads of Memory).

Among the most interesting artefacts are a carding machine, a continuous spinning machine, a warping machine, several looms from different eras and technologies, including a jacquard and a shuttleless loom.

Bolbec, known as the capital of the *vallée d'or* (golden valley), was, along with Rouen, a major centre of cotton manufacturing in France from the 17th century. Proximity to the port of Le Havre, a major cotton importation centre, a fast-flowing stream called the Rivière du Commerce (or Rivière de Bolbec), and a long tradition of spinning and weaving (flax) in Pays de Caux region contributed to this tradition.

Two main types of fabric were produced there: the popular '*rouenneries*' (checked cotton handkerchiefs and towels used by everyone in the region) and the luxurious '*indiennes*' (block-printed fabrics), which were expensive, so reserved for bourgeois customers.

Visitors are guided through the entire production process by ex-workers, and can even buy traditional Bolbec handkerchiefs made right before their eyes in the workshop.

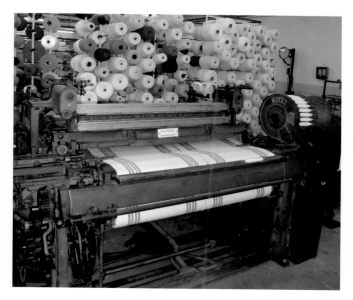

CRYPT OF
SAINT-JEAN D'ABBETOT

Normandy's richest church for mural paintings

76430 La Cerlangue
From Tancarville bridge take D910 and then D39, cross La Cerlangue with its
beautiful Église Saint-Léonard topped with stone spire
After about 800 metres, turn left towards Saint-Jean d'Abbetot (ask caretaker
who lives across the street for key to church and crypt)

The commune of Saint-Jean d'Abbetot was annexed to La Cerlangue in 1824. Visit the church, especially its Romanesque choir from the 11th century, and the crypt from the same period, to discover a hidden treasure of frescoes from the 13th and 14th centuries little known to the people of Seine-Maritime.

This marvel was on the verge of disappearing in 1835, as the church was falling into ruin. Its preservation and restoration were only made possible thanks to the determination of Abbot Cochet, archaeologist and member of the departmental commission of antiquities of what was then still called Seine-Inférieure, with the support of the prefect against the mayor. Restoration work began in 1855, carried out by a painter specialising in murals, Anatole Dauvergne.

The frescoes in the upper church and crypt, inspired by biblical scenes, are generally on the same theme: Christ in majesty surrounded by the four evangelists; other saints including James, Bartholomew, Thomas, Nicholas, St Giles and his deer.

Interestingly, the crypt is dedicated to St Martin, although he isn't depicted. The presence of a crypt at that time apparently indicated a pilgrimage to the relics of a bishop who may have shared the same name as St Jean, abbot of Deux-Jumeaux monastery in Calvados.

The church and crypt, built with Caen stone, also feature Romanesque sculpted motifs like those found in some churches in Lower Normandy, possibly inspired by Abbaye de Saint-Georges de Boscherville, to which they were connected.

TOMB OF ST HONORINA

35

A radiant saint

Prieuré de Graville
Rue Élisée Reclus – Rue de l'Abbaye
76600 Le Havre
02 35 24 51 00
musees.histoire@ville-lehavre.fr
Daily except Tues, 10am–12.30pm and 1.45pm–6pm
Free entry 1st Sat of month

Graville, a former commune annexed to Le Havre since 1824, possesses the oldest monument in the city: Graville priory, which itself houses the tomb of St Honorina in the church choir. Legend has it that in the year 303 a young virgin from Caudebec was martyred for maintaining her Christian faith at Mélamare, near the Roman settlement of Juliobona (Lillebonne). Her body was thrown into the Seine and washed ashore at the foot of Graville hill. It was then transferred to the site that would become the priory, soon to be the object of a major pilgrimage.

In the late 9th century, fearing a Viking advance, the decision was made to protect Honorina's relics. They were transferred upriver to Conflans-sur-Oise, at the confluence of the Seine and the Oise – a town that would later become Conflans-Sainte-Honorine. Miracles proliferated there, especially involving the liberation of prisoners and sailors.

After the treaty of Saint-Clair-sur-Epte in 911, when the danger had passed, Conflans returned part of these relics to Graville. The transfer was accompanied by scenes of devotion that led to the construction of a church around 1100 to house the relics, as well as a priory. The tomb of Honorina, which has been attested since 1200, is still venerated.

Graville priory, plundered by the Huguenots during the Wars of Religion of the 16th century, devastated by fire in 1787, and sold as national property in 1790, was rebuilt. The tomb of St Honorina, emptied of its relics, was rediscovered in the church choir in 1867. An opening had been made in the sarcophagus so that pilgrims could stick their heads through, as the saint's radiance is said to be transmitted to any nearby object. St Honorina is believed to assist women in childbirth and protect against miscarriages. She comes to the aid of pregnant women and fragile or disabled children. Sometimes she is even invoked for the purpose of having children. Celebrated in the dioceses of Rouen and Bayeux, she is also believed to cure deafness. The other buildings of Graville priory house a museum of religious art.

LOURDES GROTTO
AT ÉGLISE NOTRE-DAME
DE LA VICTOIRE ET DE LA PAIX

36

A peaceful place in an industrial landscape

33 Rue Gustave Nicolle – 76600 Le Havre
Open summer 7.30am–8pm, winter 7.30am–7pm
Open access
Bus No. 3 (Polygone stop)

In the heart of the Eure district of Le Havre – a multicultural and working-class neighbourhood in an industrial landscape – you

wouldn't expect to find a replica of the grotto of Massabielle in Lourdes (Hautes-Pyrénées).

The grotto, invisible from the street and unknown to most Le Havrians other than the locals who frequent it, lies behind Notre-Dame de la Victoire et de la Paix, a granite church built in 1924.

The full-scale reproduction in concrete is a peaceful place of meditation and prayer. It was designed in 1946 at the request of canon Pierre-Paul Boisseau 'in recognition of the Church's protection during the Second World War', as indicated on an explanatory panel.

The grotto with its representation of the Virgin Mary, the altar, candles, flowers and benches, is maintained by a team of dedicated volunteers who ensure a welcoming atmosphere, just as at Lourdes.

37

SALON DES NAVIGATEURS

A salon that turns heads

*Saint-François neighbourhood, corner of Rue du Petit Croissant, Rue Jean de
La Fontaine and Rue de Bretagne – 76000 Le Havre
02 35 42 12 71
Open throughout the year on reservation, Tues–Fri 10am–midday and
2.30pm–5.30pm
Please wear a mask
Admission free*

In the Saint-François neighbourhood, the Navigators' Salon is an unmissable reconstitution of a vintage hair salon. It stands at the junction of three streets, and sets the tone on the sidewalk of Rue du Petit Croissant with a dinghy, a lifebuoy, transatlantic ships, and a parasol.

Owner Daniel Lecompte has been involved with the hairdressing profession since the age of 11. Dressed in a striped T-shirt, sailor's jacket and red-pompom beret from the French Navy, he welcomes his haircut clients in what amounts to a hairdressing museum. You can admire collector's items of great interest: combs, scissors, hairdryers, beard plates, shaving brushes, bottles of cologne and perfume, clippers, razors, curlers, powder cases, photos, posters, not to mention clothing models ...

But the owner-hairdresser didn't stop at collecting such equipment. His love for the navy, which led him to sail several times on the *France* and

other ships as a replacement hairdresser for the crew, also led him to settle in Le Havre. He lives and works around Breton sailors, where throngs of sailors used to patronise his salon when their ships had extended stopovers.

In exchange for a haircut, he acquired from these regulars some of the marine objects now displayed in his museum. The eclectic collection is all the more surprising for that.

NEARBY

Only 300 metres from the Navigators' Salon, near the shipowner's house, the fish market on Quai de l'Île consists of a group of stands, some decorated with naive frescoes. The fisher folk sell their catches there on weekday afternoons.

RED COBBLESTONES
OF RUE DE PARIS

Memory of the city's founding

At intersection of Rue de Paris and Rue Richelieu
76000 Le Havre

At the intersection of Rue de Paris and Rue Richelieu, embedded in the road surface and one of the sidewalks, red cobblestones often go unnoticed by Le Havrians.

These stones, deliberately inserted into the pavement during reconstruction of the city centre in the 1950s, mark the location of the eastern tower of a gatehouse called Porte Richelieu or Porte d'Ingouville, which was part of the original fortifications.

After the foundation of a port and a trading city called Le Havre-de-Grâce in 1517 by King Francis I, Cardinal Richelieu was made governor in 1626. To protect the city, Richelieu planned a more imposing citadel on the site of the one built in 1564 by Henry II, son and successor of Francis I.

Construction of the gatehouse began in 1628 and was completed in 1632. This impressive edifice, made from cut stone and red brick, was a monumental gate, a symbol of strength and elegance, flanked by two round towers, each 28 metres high.

But the city's expansion to the north on the plain of Ingouville led to demolition in 1791 to make way for the excavation of the docks now known as Bassin du Commerce and Bassin de la Barre. The ramparts were relocated 500 metres beyond their original position.

LA PORTE D'INGOUVILLE
en 1652

RUE DURÉCU

A spectacular example of pre-war city level

Saint-Vincent neighbourhood
76600 Le Havre

Rue Durécu, formerly a private dead-end alley called Impasse Daupeley, probably named after its owner, is the Le Havre's most spectacular example of the pre-war city level. The rebuilt city centre, just a few steps away, was raised using some of the rubble from the devastating bombings of 5 and 6 September 1944. The few houses not destroyed In Rue Durécu are over a metre below the elevated level.

Access to the entrances of these still-inhabited houses is therefore via small staircases, either on either side of a narrow alley or directly in front of the building.

All these houses, several of which are constructed to the same model, date back to the late 19th century.

You can also see the pre-war city level at the city hall gardens (green spaces and fountains), at the intersection of Rue Théodore Maillant and Rue Jules Ancel.

Durécu, the 'formidable' lifeguard

Born in Ingouville, a former suburb of Le Havre, Onésime Pierre Durécu (1812–74) was a sailor and then a master hauler at the port of Le Havre.

He made 59 rescues throughout his career, saving probably more than 200 people, earning him the epithet of 'formidable' lifeguard. He was awarded the Legion of Honour for bravery in 1864 and died during his last rescue in 1874.

At the port entrance the haulers carried out some of the manoeuvres now made by tugs. The master haulers were highly respected, as they also carried out rescues at sea.

There is a monument to Durécu's memory in Sainte-Marie cemetery at Le Havre.

FERME MARINE AQUACAUX

A marine farm in a former NATO base

70 Chemin de Saint-Andrieux
76930 Octeville-sur-Mer
Visits Mon–Fri 8.30am–12.30pm and 1.30pm–5.30pm
Weekend visits, reservation only, for groups (minimum 15 people)
Guided tour 4pm (reservation strongly recommended: 02 35 46 04 97 or
aquacaux.fr)
D940 between Le Havre and Étretat, signposted from Calvaire roundabout
Parking at top of cliff

A quacaux, the impressive marine farm, is accessed by a flight of 498 steps or a 100-metre steep path that leads from the top of the cliff to sea level. The location is a former NATO pumping station from the 1960s.

The Aquacaux association, established in 1988, raises turbot with educational aims, so that visitors can understand all the stages of fish farming, especially the larval stage. Larvae are fed with zooplankton

grown on-site. The entire food chain is recreated, much to the delight of schoolchildren who can watch other marine animals in the aquariums (sea anemones, seahorses, dogfish) and even have a marine aquarium in their classroom.

Visitors can buy the turbot raised on-site, which are killed and prepared on-site as well.

The cliff still retains several spectacular remnants of the NATO installations, including a freight elevator and four 10,000-cubic-metre reservoirs connected to pumping facilities in armoured buildings that supplied two 2-km pipelines.

In the context of the Cold War in the 1960s, three wrecked ships were also sunk in front of the reservoirs to prevent attacks.

The site was abandoned by the military in 1980 and 10 years later it was taken over by the Aquacaux association, which also develops biodiversity protection and enhancement activities on the cliff and along the coast. This involves inclusion projects that allow people and the environment to rebuild, such as coastal clean-ups, ecograzing using goats and donkeys, beekeeping, preservation of natural spaces (fauna, flora, fossils …), and restoration and maintenance of buildings.

AÎTRE DE BRISGARET AT MONTIVILLIERS

A little-known masterpiece from the 16th century

From Abbaye de Montivilliers (76190), past the abbey church, take Rue Félix Faure then Rue du Faubourg Assiquet towards Fécamp
After about 700 metres turn left onto Rue Aldric Crevel
Ascend the steep slope known as 'Brisgaret' to find the hors les murs (outside the walls) cemetery on the right, its monumental entrance housing the Aître de Brisgaret
02 35 30 96 66 – abbaye-montivilliers.fr
Daily 8.30am–6pm, Easter to All Saints' Day
Unusual tours occasionally organised

Everyone knows the Saint-Maclou atrium at Rouen, a group of timber-framed buildings forming an enclosed courtyard, which from the 16th century was a charnel-house. It is now home to Rouen's École des Beaux-Arts. But very few have visited the Brisgaret atrium at Montivilliers. Sadly unfinished, it features a 36-metre wooden gallery on the western side of the cemetery. This gallery, built in the 16th century, rests on 17 posts supporting a carved-frame structure that once housed the ossuary. The atrium is completed by a chapel from the same period.

In those days skeletons didn't stay in the charnel house ground for long – just long enough to decompose. They were then transferred to the ossuary on the first floor of the atrium gallery.

Reasonable to assume, then, that these charnel houses were developed to cope with major epidemics, such as the plague that struck Europe from the 14th century onwards.

Apart from its architectural aspect, the interest of the atrium lies in the funerary woodcarvings, illustrated by each post. The main themes to be tackled are the instruments of the Passion, recalling the crucifixion of Christ on the Cross (hammer, sponge, pincers, nails, cross, crown of thorns, ladder, instruments of torture), death and its attributes (scythe, bones, hourglass, shovel, skull), and contemporary figures illustrating the transition from life to demise (figure wrapped in a shroud with feet in a tomb, skeleton frolicking or carrying a scythe, terrified man draped in a cloak, knight with a sword at his back). The whole thing constitutes a 16th-century masterpiece of carpentry well worth discovering.

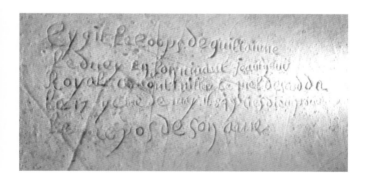

The word *aître* comes from the Latin *atrium*. In ancient Rome it referred to a square or rectangular courtyard surrounded by buildings.

ÉTRETAT GARDENS

Contemporary gardens offering a unique panorama of the sea

Avenue Damilaville, 76790 Étretat
02 35 27 05 76
info@etretatgarden.fr
Daily mid-Feb–mid-Dec 10am–7pm
The best way to reach garden, on top of Amont cliff, if you prefer not to climb up on foot, is to take tourist train from centre of Étretat – parking spaces about 25 to 30 min walk from garden
There is a drop-off point in front of garden entrance near Chapelle des Marins

Designed in 2015 by talented Russian landscape designer Alexandre Grivko, the spectacular gardens of Étretat are still relatively unknown. Here nature, architecture and contemporary art speak to one another. These gardens on top of Amont cliff in Étretat, inspired by the techniques used by landscape architect Le Nôtre at the Palace of

Versailles, offer a unique perspective on the famous contours of the Côte d'Albâtre.

In 1903 actress Madame Thébault had the villa Roxelane built on this land, as a tribute to the slave who became the wife of Ottoman Sultan Suleiman the Magnificent, since playing that role had made her famous. She commissioned local landscape architect Auguste Lecanu to design an Impressionist-inspired garden where she welcomed her friend Claude Monet, a visit commemorated with a bamboo sculpture by Wictor Szostalo. Captivated by the charm of the place, Alexandre Grivko bought Roxelane a few years ago, doubled the size of the original garden, and decided to create a land-art garden against the strong conservationist background of Étretat.

Taking time to visit and explore the different parts of the garden is recommended: the Garden of Avatars, Parnassus, the Garden of Embraces and Trees, the Garden of Emotions, the Garden of the Elements, the Orchid Garden, and the Nature Garden. Each section presents a unique approach to the treatment of plants, carefully selected for their resistance to salty sea spray, seamlessly blending topiary and contemporary artwork. They evoke the rolling waves on the beach or form arches of greenery reminiscent of the Porte d'Aval. The gardens are populated with expressive figures by sculptor Samuel Salcedo, which appear like raindrops fallen upon these meticulously maintained gardens, tended year-round by gardeners trained by their designer.

Winners of the European Garden Award in the category of 'Enhancement of a Historical Garden' and holding the 'Remarkable Garden' label, the gardens of Étretat are a highly successful poetic marriage of contemporary art and grandiose nature.

FISH SMOKEHOUSE
ON FÉCAMP'S GRAND QUAI

Smoked like a Fécamp local

16 Grand Quai – 76400 Fécamp
02 35 10 60 96
ville-fecamp.fr
Visits: contact Maison du Patrimoine at 10 Rue des Forts

'*Boucané comme un Fécampois*' is the saying inherited by workers at the *boucanes*, the local term for fish smokehouses. This is a method of preserving fish by smoking it in large chimneys called *boucanes*, where the fire was covered with fresh beech chips to produce smoke that flavoured the herring while it was cooking.

In the 1930s golden age of smoked herring, known as *saffate* or *bouffi*, which fed the Normans, Fécamp was the smokehouse centre. There were over 300 of them, recognisable by numerous chimney stacks rising from the gables. The last remaining smokehouse, the Prentout, now called the Boucane du Grand Quai or Grande Boucane, can be visited on certain occasions as part of a tour called *Fécamp capitale des terre-neuvas* – capital of the Newfoundlanders – organised by the Maison du Patrimoine.

In addition, during Fécamp's Fête du Hareng (Herring Festival), which takes place annually at the end of November, the Boucane du Grand Quai is the focal point of a re-enactment of herring preparation and smoking by former workers reviving the gestures they made throughout their working lives.

NEARBY

Another old but less spectacular smokehouse still sits right next door, at No. 12 Grand Quai, in the bar-restaurant La Boucane.

To find out more about smokehouses, try watching these two films: *La Boucane*, filmed by Jean Gaumy in 1985, and *Les Femmes aux poissons*, directed by Alexandre Lefrançois in 2002.

ALPHABETICAL INDEX BY TOWN

ACKNOWLEDGEMENTS

Jean-Christophe Collet:

Special thanks to the Manche and Orne departmental committees, my fellow journalists, the Basse-Normandie tourist offices and the various volunteer contributors.

Alain Joubert:

Calvados: Caroline Barray, Christine Van Daele et Florence Marie.

Eure: Dominique Krauskopf; Michèle Age; Éric Catherine; Jean-Pierre Leroux; Suzanne Lipinska; Laurent Guyard; Hubert Labrouche; Mme Brard; Séverine Saillour-Caudroit; Florence Calame-Levert; Direction des sites et musées départementaux de la Seine-Maritime; Jacques Loiseau; Luc Bonnin; Anne and Jean-François Durand; Denis Goudenhooft; Jacques Langlois; Tourist office for the canton of Quillebeuf in Bourneville; Tourist office of Cormeilles; Gérard Briavoine; Sandra Lefrançois; Tourist office of Saint-Georges-du-Vièvre; Mauricette de Colombel; Maryvonne Mameaux; Éliane Benoit-Gonin; Restaurant *Ancien hôtel Baudy* in Giverny; Caroline Roudet; Virginie Allard; Armel Feuillet and Alain Kempynck; Jacqueline Caffin; Frédéric Lamblin; Dr F. Dubosc; Pierre Roussel; Anne-Sophie Auger-Sergent.

Seine-Maritime: Dominique Krauskopf; Michèle age; Benoît Eliot and Stéphane Rioland, Éditions Point de vues; Institution Saint-Joseph, Mesnières-en-Bray; Jacques and Juliette Damville; Michel Lerond; Élisabeth Leprêtre; Association 'Bolbec au fil de la Mémoire'; Jean-Pierre Leroux; 'Chêne'; Frédéric Toussaint; Anne-Marie C. Damamme; Departmental Sites and Museums Directorate from Seine-Maritime; Patrice Perrier; Association Pacific-Vapeur-Club; Catherine Sauvage, Alliance et Culture; Philippe Dupont; Henri Decaens; Tourist office of Rouen; Alain Alexandre; Tourist office of Forges-les-Eaux; Simtof; Samuel Craquelin; Tourist office of Le Havre; Daniel Lecompte; Association des amis de la chapelle de Saint-Adrien; Lieutenant-colonel Jean-Pierre Collinet; Musée du Prieuré in Harfleur; Maison du Patrimoine in Fécamp; Jacques Bardel; Martine Pastor; Lucette Aubourg; Enzo Mutarelli; Jean-Yves Merle; Jean-Paul Herbert; Arlette Dubois; Geoff Troll; Jean-Yves Picard; Tourist office of Le Tréport; Tourist office of Mers-les-Bains; Jacques Tanguy.

Éditions Jonglez: Marie-Odile Alline, Dominique Cabuil, Chantal Lecomte, Violaine and Jean-François Lion, Kees and Marie-Aude van Beek.

PHOTO CREDITS

Cover photo: Matheo JBT on Unsplash.

Manche – Orne – Calvados: all photos by **Jean-Christophe Collet** except:

Manche: Tour of Grottes de Jobourg: Cyril Forafo (Expsen) – Graffiti in Morsalines and Quettehou churches: Langlois – Matthieu Angot's garden: Mathieu Angot – Trochlight stroll in Villedieu-les-Poêles: Tourist office of Villedieu-les-Poêles.

Orne: Forgiveness for motorists: photo from the organisers – Musée des Commerces et des Marques: Tourist office of Tourouvre

Calvados: 'Droues' of Port-en-Bessin: photo Guillaume – Maison bleue: Maison bleue Association – Greenwich Meridian in Villers: tourist office of Villers-sur-Mer – Chapelle Saint-Vigor: © Jacques Basile – La Forge home workshop: ©DR.

Eure – Seine-Maritime: all photos by **Alain Joubert** except:

Eure: Boat graffiti at Quillebeuf: Relevés Henri Cahingt – Model of the *Télémaque*: based on an original drawing by Captain Adrien Quemin – Auction of the candles (p. 190): Yohann Deslandes, photographer for the Seine-Maritime departmental museums – Vows at Chapelle Saint-Thomas, Saint-Clair bonfire at La Haye-de-Routot, Chapelle de la Ronce, Bridge towpath window: Michèle Lesage – Orties Folies festival: Jean-Pierre Leroux – Legends of Abbaye de Mortemer: Photo E. Catherine – Château de Bizy *pediluvium*: Thomas Jonglez – Restaurant of former Hôtel Baudy: photo of the owners – Musée des instruments à vent: Musée des instruments à vent, Couture-Boussey – Musée de l'écorché d'anatomie: Musée de l'écorché d'anatomie, Le Neubourg.

Seine-Maritime: Festival du Lin et de l'Aiguille: Catherine Sauvage – Woodcutter's hut in Eawy forest: Alain Gracia – Ferme de Bray, La Closerie english-style gardens: Dominique Krauskopf – Bread oven of La Pannevert, Angélique du Coudray's 'ghost': Élodie Laval – Masonic symbolism of tomb of cardinals of Amboise, Maison de l'Annonciation, Tour de la Pucelle, Atomic shelter of Seine-Maritime Conseil Général, Saint-Jean-d'Abetot crypt: VMA   Masonic symbolism of tomb of cardinals of Amboise (p. 276): Raimond Sepkking – Pacific Vapeur Club locomotive: Pacific-Vapeur-Club, Marcel Delrue – Graffiti at Manoir du Catel (p. 310): Catherine Beudaert – Allouville-Bellefosse oak (p. 312): drawing from Louis-François age, Public library, Rouen – Atelier-musée du textile de Bolbec: Jean-Pierre Leroux – Lourdes grotto at Église Notre-Dame de la Victoire et de la Paix, Red cobblestones of Rue de Paris, Rue Durécu: Marie-Odile Boitout – Étretat gardens: Richard Bloom (p. 338) ; Fish smokehouse on Fécamp's Grand Quai: Service Patrimoine-Ville de Fécamp.

TEXTS

All texts by **Jean-Christophe Collet** (Manche, Orne, Calvados) and **Alain Joubert** (Eure, Seine Maritime, Maison-atelier La Forge dans le Calvados), except:

– Riddle of Église de Saint-Grégoire-du-Vièvre facade – Mysterious graffiti of the prisoner's tower – Templar symboles in Église Saint-Gervais-et-Saint-Protais – Knights Templar: myths and reality – Église de Saint-Martin stalls – Occult marks and symbols at Église Saint-Pierre – Operative Freemasonry and the Royal Art – Masonic symbolism of tomb of cardinals of Amboise - Maison de l'Annonciation: VMA.
– Festival du Lin et de l'Aiguille – Ferme de Bray – La Closerie English-style gardens: Dominique Krauskopf.
– Tour de la Pucelle, Atomic shelter of Seine-Maritime Conseil Général, Napoleon column: Marie Painblanc-Obre.
– Bread oven of La Pannevert, Angélique du Coudray's 'ghost': Élodie Laval.
– Château de Bizy *pediluvium*: Thomas Jonglez.
– Lourdes grotto at Église Notre-Dame de la Victoire et de la Paix, Red cobblestones of Rue de Paris, Rue Durécu, Statue of St Louis: Marie-Odile Boitout.

Cartography: **Cyrille Suss** – Layout: **Emmanuelle Willard Toulemonde** – Translation: **Sonny Alexander** – Copy-editing: **Caroline Lawrence** – Proofreading: **Lee Dickinson** – Publishing: **Clémence Mathé**.

Thomas Jonglez

It was September 1995 and Thomas Jonglez was in Peshawar, the northern Pakistani city 20 kilometres from the tribal zone he was to visit a few days later. It occurred to him that he should record the hidden aspects of his native city, Paris, which he knew so well. During his seven-month trip back home from Beijing, the countries he crossed took in Tibet (entering clandestinely, hidden under blankets in an overnight bus), Iran and Kurdistan. He never took a plane but travelled by boat, train or bus, hitchhiking, cycling, on horseback or on foot, reaching Paris just in time to celebrate Christmas with the family.

On his return, he spent two fantastic years wandering the streets of the capital to gather material for his first 'secret guide', written with a friend. For the next seven years he worked in the steel industry until the passion for discovery overtook him. He launched Jonglez Publishing in 2003 and moved to Venice three years later.

In 2013, in search of new adventures, the family left Venice and spent six months travelling to Brazil, via North Korea, Micronesia, the Solomon Islands, Easter Island, Peru and Bolivia.

After seven years in Rio de Janeiro, he now lives in Berlin with his wife and three children.

Jonglez Publishing produces a range of titles in nine languages, released in 40 countries.

© JONGLEZ 2024
Registration of copyright: April 2024 – Edition: 01
ISBN: 978-2-36195-730-8
Printed in Bulgaria by Dedrax